Barbara in the Bodleian:
Revelations from the Pym Archives

Barbara in the Bodleian:
Revelations from the Pym Archives

Yvonne Cocking

The Barbara Pym Society
Oxford and Boston

Barbara in the Bodleian:
Revelations from the Pym Archives

Copyright ©2013 by The Barbara Pym Society

Printed in Great Britain

ISBN 978-0-615-76566-2

The Barbara Pym Society
barbarapymsociety@gmail.com
St Hilda's College
Oxford OX4 1DY
UK

www.barbara-pym.org

Contents

Preface

This book is a tribute to two remarkable women, both of who have spent a considerable amount of time in Oxford's Bodleian Library.

The first, of course, is Barbara Pym, whose centenary we celebrate in 2013. She spent many hours in 'the Bod.' while an undergraduate at St Hilda's in the early 1930s, reading, doing research, writing in her journal, and stalking various young men, including 'Lorenzo' (Henry Harvey). In June 1971 she wrote to Philip Larkin,

> The (then) English Reading Room of the Bodleian Library has many sentimental memories for me – I can remember deliberately *not* going there for fear of seeing a certain person or to hope that my absence would be noted.

After Barbara's death, her diaries, notebooks, manuscripts, correspondence, and other papers were donated to the Bodleian, where they are housed in the Department of Special Collections and Western Manuscripts. While Hazel Holt and Hilary Pym Walton have already shared excerpts from Barbara's journals and correspondence in *A Very Private Eye,* this collection of essays introduces a great deal of new material. It sheds more light on her life, character, and creative process, and will therefore be welcomed both by literary critics and scholars, and by Barbara's many devoted readers.

The second 'excellent woman' is Yvonne Cocking, who since 2001 has prepared and presented twelve research papers at conferences of the Barbara Pym Society, both in the U.K. and the U.S., as well as combing the archives for poems, short stories, and other unpublished material to present as dramatised readings or to publish in the Society's semi-annual journal, *Green Leaves.* There is undoubtedly no one more intimately acquainted with the riches of the Pym archives than Yvonne, and this book is a testimonial to her devotion to Barbara and her loyal fans.

When I first considered the possibility of combining Yvonne's research papers into a monograph, I thought it might be a special centenary issue of *Green Leaves*. It quickly became apparent that there was enough material to completely fill at least four issues of our 16-page newsletter, and indeed there was enough for a book of around 250 pages – exactly the length of a typical Pym novel.

All of the novels published during Barbara's lifetime are examined in this collection. Five of the papers were presented at Annual General Meetings of the Society at St Hilda's College, Oxford, between 2000 and 2010, seven were presented at North American conferences in Cambridge, Massachusetts, between 2005 and 2012, and chapters 6 and 12 were written especially for this volume.

Thomas Sopko

Cambridge, Massachusetts
January 2013

The Barbara Pym Society

In August 1993 a Barbara Pym Literary Weekend was held at St Hilda's College, Oxford, as part of the College's Centenary celebrations, with 120 people in attendance. As a result of this enthusiastic gathering, the Barbara Pym Society was founded on 15 April 1994, with 165 people enrolled as either Honorary Life Members or Founder Members. The Society is administered through St Hilda's College, where Barbara took her BA in English Language and Literature in 1934.

The Society presently has approximately 500 members and holds its Annual General Meeting at St Hilda's every September. In addition, the Society holds a spring meeting in London, and the annual North American Conference is held in March in Cambridge, Massachusetts. *Green Leaves*, the Society's newsletter, is published twice yearly.

The aims of the Society are to foster the appreciation and wider knowledge of the life and works of Barbara Pym; to secure the preservation of the manuscripts, letters and memorabilia of Barbara Pym in conjunction with the Bodleian Library; to encourage and support publications and theses on Barbara Pym, her life and work; and to provide a programme of literary events and regular communications concerning the work of Barbara Pym.

More information about the Society and its activities may be found online at www.barbara-pym.org

Acknowledgements

Along with being immensely grateful to Yvonne Cocking for her years of painstaking research and selfless devotion to the cause, I would also like to thank the following members of the Barbara Pym Society for their assistance with this project:

Hazel Holt, Barbara's dear friend and literary executor, for her encouragement and assistance, and for writing the foreword;

Lloyd Miller for designing the typography, graphics, and cover;

Kathy Ackley and Christine Shuttleworth for proofreading; and

Hazel Bell for undertaking 'the arduous and thankless task' of preparing the index.

Foreword

Barbara said 'There's a new girl in the Library.' There frequently was. I'd been one myself, joining the International African Institute in 1950 for no other reason than that I needed a job in London and nothing else seemed to be available. Since my only experience of libraries was as a reader, Ruth Jones, the formidable Librarian, on my first day set me the task of putting sticky labels onto the spines of books, like Caro in *An Academic Question*. Yvonne, the new girl in question was, however, the real thing and perfectly at home in the world of the 5x3 catalogue card, bibliographies, and other library mysteries. She brought to the Institute's Library a welcome efficiency and professionalism.

All Yvonne's gifts have made her the perfect Archivist to the Barbara Pym Society. Many hours spent in Room 132 of the New Bodleian (in early days under Colin Harris, and later Judith Priestman, a sort of unofficial Pym Club) means that she has a unique knowledge of the wealth of material collected there. This, and the fact that she knew Barbara, has given her a special insight into the many and varied items.

Yvonne also had the brilliant idea of making dramatic adaptations of the novels to be performed by Members at the annual Conferences, along with readings of the unpublished short stories. She also gave papers, at Oxford and at Boston, on different aspects of Barbara's life and times, inspired by her minute examination of the riches in the Bodleian. These papers, with some additions, notably extracts from reviews and comments from friends and fans, are a valuable contribution to the many books on Barbara, and it is important that they should be published for the benefit not only of Members of the Society, but also for those who did not have the opportunity of hearing them in their original form.

The fact that they were originally read aloud means that the research that inspired them is presented in a notably clear and agreeable style. The voice of the writer comes through, making it, refreshingly, a personal as well as a scholarly work. It is a work of enthusiasm and affection which will give information and pleasure to all Barbara's admirers.

Hazel Holt

Chard, Somerset
January 2013

1

Barbara and I at the International African Institute

1963 – 1967

There seem to be more staff in the Library
than anywhere else – I suppose
their purpose is to discourage Visitors.

1

Barbara and I at the
International African Institute

In 1960 I returned to England after ten years in Northern Rhodesia (Zambia), where for some of that time I had been in charge of the Record Library of the Central African Broadcasting Station in Lusaka. I had passed the elementary examinations in two of the local languages, Chibemba and Chinyanja; no doubt this looked good on my CV when I applied for an assistant librarian's job at the International African Institute (IAI) in London, which I was offered. I was introduced to all the staff, including Barbara Pym, the assistant editor of the journal *Africa*, who, other colleagues told me, had had six novels published, but whose type of book was now out of favour. I started reading the novels, but, I'm afraid, like so many young people in the 1960s, I did not find them very exciting. The Institute itself, with its charismatic director Daryll Forde, I did find interesting, as I had much enjoyed my time in Africa and had read many books on the subject.

By the beginning of the twentieth century the work of ethnologists (cultural anthropologists) was being conducted in a more systematic manner than heretofore, and was consequently being taken more seriously by the politicians back in England. Even before the First World War the Colonial Office was beginning to think that it ought to know more about African customs. After all, Sir Frederick Hodgson, Governor of the Gold Coast, nearly lost his life in 1900 because he offended the Paramount Chief through his ignorance of the sacred role of the Golden Stool in Ashanti culture! According to one source, the Colonial Office decided that 'African customs were to be accorded some respect instead of being studied simply to change them into European ones.[1]'

The famous anthropologist Sir Edward Evans-Pritchard was given special facilities for his work among the Azande and Nuer peoples in the

Sudan, and from 1909 to 1915 Northcote W. Thomas received government support for anthropological study in Nigeria. In 1926 the International African Institute in London was founded by Sir Frederick Lugard (later 1st Baron Lugard), a soldier and administrator who had served in many parts of the Empire, including the Sudan, Nyasaland and Uganda, finally becoming Governor General of Nigeria. The purpose of the Institute was to coordinate the ethnological and linguistic studies of sub-Saharan Africa, where Belgium, France, Germany and Portugal, the main colonists after England, all had physical and cultural anthropologists working in the field. After World War II the Institute was revitalised by Daryll Forde, Professor of Anthropology at University College London. At that time there were about 25 anthropologists working in British colonial Africa on government grants.

To further its aims, the Institute had a considerable publishing programme, including a quarterly journal entitled *Africa*, which contained reports of original work from the field, conference news, book reviews and so on; two series, the *Ethnographic Survey of Africa* and the *Linguistic Survey of Africa*, which updated the subjects from time to time; and occasional monographs. In 1946 Barbara joined the Institute's staff as an editorial assistant on these publications. Later she was to become the Assistant Editor of *Africa* and the *Surveys*. Later there was another quarterly publication, *African Abstracts*, edited by Hazel Holt with considerable input from the library staff, who constituted two-fifths of the total complement.

I joined the IAI as a library assistant early in 1963. The offices were in St Dunstan's Chambers, Fetter Lane, off Fleet Street. The chief claim of this undistinguished building was that Dryden had once lived here, and as Barbara noted in her diary, she and Hazel Holt liked to think that *Absalom and Achitophel* might have been written there! The doorway opened on to a wide flight of brown lino-covered stairs, and the offices were on the first and second floors of the building. As I recall, the staff at that time consisted of the Professor, two senior administration staff (ladies), and Barbara and her assistant Hazel on the upper floor; and on the lower, the Librarian and three staff, and a bookkeeper.

At the top of the stairs, a door on the right led into the library, a suite of three rooms, all overlooking Fetter Lane. To the left was the reading room, and on the right a room divided into two, for the librarian and a filing clerk. The centre room saw most of the activity. The greater part of the three walls was occupied by wooden card filing cabinets beneath which unbound journals were stored in boxes specially made to fit a wide variety of journal sizes. Beneath the windows my colleague and I faced each other across large desks, with the big typewriters of the day in front of us and surrounded by galley and page proofs and other impedimenta of library duties. And, of course, overflowing ashtrays – most of us smoked in those days. All visitors came here first, and part of my job was to help them to find the information they sought, or to pass them on to the appropriate staff member, the Librarian herself preferring not to deal with readers. Apart from the usual library routine of entering journal receipts, dealing with our small collection of books and so on, our main task was to prepare entries for *African Abstracts*. To this end, we made analytical entries, and the appropriate added entries for every article within our subject fields from every journal we took, and also for every reference cited in these articles if we did not have them already. In pursuit of these fugitive items I had to traipse around various other institutions, like the Royal Anthropological Institute and the School of Oriental and African Studies, to obtain copies or at least to verify their authenticity. Our catalogue was really a bibliography, since it contained entries for some material we did not actually hold, and was disproportionately large for the size of the collection. In fact, several years later I believe that the weight of these cabinets was exerting such stress on the floor that they had to be moved around in order to distribute the weight more evenly and avoid an imminent collapse!

I did not see Barbara very often as our areas of work did not overlap much, and when they did Hazel was the usual intermediary. Bringing us books they didn't want to review, or coming to check a reference, or reporting the possible arrival of a VIP, Hazel came down to see us for a few minutes most days, visits which I and my fellow worker much enjoyed as Hazel had a gift for investing the slightest piece of news with a dramatic quality.

However, I do have a clear mental picture of Barbara sitting in her office upstairs, one arm draped over the back of another chair with a cigarette in hand, on her lips the 'warm, crooked smile' that Nancy Ellen Talburt noted in her May 2000 article in *Green Leaves*. She seemed to me always to have an air of calm confidence about her – despite the chaotic appearance of her desk, strewn with manuscripts and proofs. She spoke in measured tones, enunciating very clearly, never rushing her words or raising her voice suddenly. To me she was an authoritative, slightly awe-inspiring figure, partly because she was my senior in status as well as age, but also because she was a novelist, the first I had met. She was, however, very kind and non-condescending to junior staff, and received a deal of respect in return.

There are only a few references to the library in *A Very Private Eye*, and these are mostly in letters to Philip Larkin. She mentioned to him that *An Unsuitable Attachment* has a librarian in it: 'Of course, only in a small way – the library is rather like ours at the IAI – not to be compared with University libraries and their problems.'

In January 1964, the subject arose again: 'This leads me to speak of our library and what the staff do. There seem to be more staff in the library than anywhere else – I suppose their purpose is to discourage visitors'. This rather cynical remark may have been occasioned by the fact that the Librarian was reluctant to let 'Outsiders,' e.g. journalists, commercial companies and other non-academics, use the library, and wanted to charge them a fee to do so. I was rather against this and did my best to oppose it, and the matter was, I think, eventually dropped. Barbara continued, 'We don't buy a great many books, but have good holdings of foreign periodicals, some being exchanged with *Africa*. I have sometimes thought of writing a Pinterish play about our library.' I think this shows that Barbara was keeping a close, if unobtrusive, eye on the library, in which she found a rich source of comic situations.

Later that year she wrote to Philip Larkin,

> Our library has been made slightly more interesting – in a macabre way – by a rather peculiar young man joining the staff. He doesn't come in till 10.35 most mornings, and is given to

cryptic utterances which one can only half hear. I don't have much to do with him myself but hear all this from the other staff. I find it pleasanter to observe these things rather than actually participate in them.

This strange person replaced my former much-liked colleague who had, sadly as far as I was concerned, emigrated to Australia. He was very difficult to work with. I don't think he liked being told what to do by a woman only slightly older than himself – in fact I don't think he liked women much at all. He rarely made eye contact or addressed me directly, and was indeed given to semi-audible mumbling. No doubt Barbara would have heard from Hazel of his violent reaction, storming out of the room muttering as he went, when Hazel made some humorously disparaging remark to me in his hearing about the new Prime Minister [Harold Wilson] the day after the 1964 General Election!

Some months later Barbara continued the story:

Our library problem, I mean the peculiar young man, seems to have been solved. At least, he was given the sack after Christmas, being told, I believe, that there was to be some 'staff reorganization.' Is that always how it's done? Then a woman of uncertain age [the library clerk, who spent most of her day filing the innumerable catalogue cards we churned out] suddenly seemed to be sixty and she had to retire, and for a time it seemed as if nobody would come. But now there is a young girl – here I stopped writing yesterday, I suppose because I was seeing the procession of young girls over the years and perhaps got thinking that it's only the older, duller and more reliable members of the staff who go on and on.

Again in September 1969, 'We continue to have trouble in staffing our library at the Institute. A Ghanaian we had was not a success and spent a large part of his day conducting endless telephone calls in his native language (Fanti, I think).'

I left the Institute in mid-1965, made a couple of working visits in 1967, but lost all contact when I came to live in Oxfordshire in 1970. In 1977 when *Quartet in Autumn* was published I read it with great interest, not only because it was Barbara's first novel for many years, but also because I thought I might recognize the originals of the fictional characters. The identity of the men is most puzzling. Where could she have known such people? She had been at the IAI for 28 years, working mainly alongside women; the men I've already mentioned were surely non-starters. Hazel Holt tells me that after I left there was a man who worked in the library and sometimes did odd proofreading jobs for the editorial department. She writes that 'he was middle aged, with a caustic tongue, had A Mother and actually ate his lunchtime sandwiches with a knife and fork.' Where else could she have come across Norman and Edwin? Are they entirely figments of her imagination? I don't think so. I heard Hilary Walton say that Barbara's characters were an amalgam of characteristics from several sources, and were rarely obviously recognizable as 'real' people. My own conclusion is that the quartet were all based on women she had observed at work, very likely in the library where the turnover was greatest. After all, Norman and Edwin are not aggressively masculine, indeed they might be somewhat unkindly described as 'old women' themselves, and it would only have taken a little tweaking by an expert like Barbara to make female into male characters.

I conclude my short and regrettably patchy story with a few notable dates: in March 1972 the Institute moved its offices to 210 High Holborn. In May 1973 Professor Forde died and it was some months before a new young director was appointed. In November 1973 St Dunstan's Chambers was pulled down, and in summer of the next year Barbara retired to Finstock with Hilary, returning for her retirement party in December 1974. In November 1977 *Quartet in Autumn* was shortlisted for the Booker Prize, and Barbara Pym's career as a novelist was successfully re-launched.

An earlier version of this paper was presented at the 2000 Annual General Meeting in Oxford.

2

Researching Barbara Pym
in the Bodleian Library

2000 – 2013

What I personally value most are nearly
40 small notebooks…in which I since 1948
or thereabouts kept a kind of diary,
not only of events and emotions but also of
bits and ideas for novels.

Researching Barbara Pym in the Bodleian Library

'Barbara Pym, Libraries and Librarians' was the theme of the Barbara Pym Society's 2000 AGM in Oxford. One of the papers was given by Angela Carritt, at that time an assistant librarian at St Hilda's, who had previously been in the Modern Manuscripts room at the Bodleian, where she had carried out conservation work on the Pym papers. She described the processes involved in preparing manuscripts for readers' use, and the four categories into which the Pym papers had been divided, namely, Literary Papers and Notebooks, Diaries, Correspondence, and Miscellaneous Papers. This was the first most of us had heard about the content of the Pym archive, though a detailed account of these papers had been given by Anne Wyatt-Brown in her critical biography of Barbara Pym.[1] After the conference, Dr Judith Priestman of the Department of Western Manuscripts at the Bodleian Library and Librarian in charge of the Barbara Pym papers offered to show a small group of Society members a selection of them.

A visit to the Clarendon Building in Broad Street, opposite the New Bodleian, was arranged for 15 December 2000. Owing to bad weather and the date being so near to the busy Christmas holiday, it was attended by only five or six people. This small number turned out to be an advantage, as we were able to view the material with great ease in a somewhat restricted space. Because we did not have library passes we could not enter the library itself, so Dr Priestman had arranged for her selected material to be sent to the Delegates' Room in the Clarendon Building.

Among the documents chosen by Dr Priestman for the visiting group were:

The Magic Diamond (1922), Barbara's earliest recorded work

Young Men in Fancy Dress (1929-30), a novel in imitation of

Aldous Huxley's *Crome Yellow*. Barbara sent this to Robert Liddell in 1936; he described it as 'a treasure for a research worker doing a B. Litt, or surely it would be worth a D. Phil.'

Notes and drafts of *Excellent Women, The Lime Tree Bower* (afterwards called *A Glass of Blessings*), and *No Fond Return of Love*

Barbara's undergraduate diary for 1932

Correspondence with Philip Larkin and Robert Liddell

Henry Harvey's *Gerard Langbaine the Younger* (B. Litt. thesis, 1937), which Barbara had typed. This, of course, does not form part of Barbara's archive, but belongs in the Library's thesis collection.

We were all delighted with what we saw, and particularly with the correspondence between Barbara and Philip Larkin. After the meeting, several of us repaired to Blackwell's coffee shop across the road for a chat about how to proceed.

At our committee meeting in January, I gave a verbal report. In the meantime I had been in correspondence with Dr Priestman, who was very encouraging as she thought that a good deal of the material in the Archive could readily be used for publication in *Green Leaves*, especially the short stories and perhaps the poems. So I said to the Committee that I thought that someone should follow this up. In the long pause that ensued, I proposed myself. I had no exceptional qualifications for research, but I live within 15 miles of Oxford, and proximity is a prerequisite in such a situation. But, of course, librarianship is a form of research, and was particularly so in the days of 'hand searching', before the widespread use of computers, and I had a lot of experience of this.

Eileen Roberts wrote a letter to the Director of Admissions recommending that I be given a reader's ticket, and I duly presented myself again at the Clarendon Building.

However, I must mention that this was not my first acquaintance with the Bodleian Library. When I was researching *The British in Africa* in the late 1960s I had used the Rhodes House Library. When I took up the post of Librarian at the Medical Research Council's Radiobiology

Unit at Harwell, the site of the Atomic Energy Research Establishment, in October 1970, I found in my desk a ticket entitling the holder of my post to the use of the Radcliffe Science Library, the Bodleian's science collection, and even to recommend members of the unit's staff to do the same! Such power! Since the subject of my collection was narrow, we were already well supplied with significant books and journals, so I did not need to visit the Radcliffe very often.

In the past, however, when the subject was new and there was no really suitable vehicle, articles on radiobiology appeared in a range of journals, some of them quite obscure, not all of which were in our collection. So when there was a postal workers' strike for several weeks early in 1971, with no incoming or outgoing mail, I found the time to deal with some backlog of work, and decided to go to the RSL to seek out these elusive papers.

I don't remember how successful my visit was in that respect. My abiding memory is of seeing for the first time a joke which is now very old, politically incorrect, and probably best forgotten, scratched on one of the oak desks. I was horrified less by the sentiment of the joke than the desecration within those hallowed walls.

Some time in the 1980s (the Thatcher era, and the end of getting anything for nothing) I received a letter from the Bodleian to say that my reader's card was now obsolete and that I would have to apply for a new one, for which there would be a charge. To the Clarendon, then, for the first time, to find a lengthy queue, very slow-moving as the photographic equipment was out of order.

I whiled away the time talking to the applicant in front of me – an academic lady from an American university who was doing some research for a thesis on Charles I, the English monarch who reigned from 1625 until he was beheaded in 1649, and I eventually came away with a reader's card permitting 12 visits over the next year at a cost of £10, I seem to remember.

So, back to the Clarendon again in 2001 to get another ticket. The Admissions Officer asked if I had ever had one before, and when I told her what I have just told you she went to a box containing those 5" x 3" index cards, used in such quantity by libraries in the past, and found my name and details left there about 15 years earlier! She then issued me with a four-year ticket, for which, this time, owing to my age, I did not have to pay.

The group which had been on the introductory visit had thought at first of attempting something on the Pym/Larkin correspondence theme. However, when I considered that all Larkin's letters to Pym had already appeared in Anthony Thwaite's book, that all sorts of permissions would probably have to be sought for any further work, and that in any case such a project was beyond the competence of those who might be engaged on it, I decided instead, as Judith Priestman suggested, to have a look at the unpublished poems and short stories. I was hoping to find a piece that could be reprinted in the very next issue of *Green Leaves*, to provide something new and different for our readers.

As soon as my ticket was issued, I went across to the Modern Manuscripts Reading Room (Room 132), where I found that Judith had ordered up for me MS. Pym 97, Poetry and Prose from 1937, which we had looked at briefly earlier.

The first item in it is *The Sad Story of Alphonse: a warning to would-be poets*, written in February 1930, which I later learnt appeared in the Huyton Girls School magazine later that year when Barbara would have been in the Sixth Form, but neither this nor the other prose pieces seemed right for my purpose. Nor could I see a suitable context in which most of the poems could be used. There are some longish ones, dedicated to an early pre-Oxford friend, and a few short ones, three of which have since been reprinted in *Green Leaves*, when we found a suitable occasion; there is a parody of Alexander Pope, in rhyming couplets of course, and some 'fragments' like this rather poignant piece, 'inspired by Tennyson' and written after the Julian Amery episode,

> Oh that 'twere possible
> After long grief and pain
> To find the arms of the younger son of the Rt. Hon. L.S. Amery, MP
> Around me once again.

and bits of doggerel like this, written in February 1933:

> Isn't it sad
> Lorenzo is quite mad!
> He is running up and down the Iffley Road,
> All painted with woad!

For my second visit, I ordered up MSS 93 and 94 from the first section of the archived papers, wherein most of the short stories are contained. This material looked much more promising. Of the 27 or so short stories Barbara wrote, only six have been published, three posthumously, two of them in *Civil to Strangers,* the other two in that volume being reprints.

I read all the unpublished ones over several sessions, making notes on the subjects and their suitability for *Green Leaves*, and came up with four I thought could stand without any amendment. I felt 'An Afternoon Visit' (undated, but thought to be early) was the slightest – quite a sweet story but with very little dramatic impact. If it was to be included at all, it should appear first, I thought, and be followed by others with a stronger story line.

These were 'The German Baron' (1930s), 'The Pilgrimage' (1952), and 'Poor Mildred' (also from the 50s).

When I had obtained Hazel Holt's permission and Hilary Walton's enthusiastic support, these stories appeared in that order in *Green Leaves* between 2001 and 2004. Since then my researches have been dictated by the subjects of our Oxford and North American conferences.

I found the Literary Notebooks, which form a part of the first section of Barbara's archived papers, a rich source of information on the background to some of her works, though there is disappointingly little on others. She jotted down in these small books, which cover the years 1948-1979, her spontaneous thoughts, suggesting and rejecting certain ideas, and gradually developing her themes. She also recorded scenes she witnessed and conversations she overheard, some of which are recognisable in novels published later. She said herself in her Radio 3 talk *Finding a Voice* that she used notebooks to record 'possible scenes or turns of plot for novels, quotations that appeal to me, occasional over-heard scraps of conversation, anything...' and she gave this example from one of them:

> In September 1948 I described a visit to Buckfast Abbey: 'much commercialized, teas, car park, etc., shop full of Catholic junk as well as books...not thus would one be sentimentally converted to Rome, though perhaps rationally. Very young priests in the parties of sightseers, mostly in pairs like little black beetles, from the seminary at Paignton...the monk show-ing us round says "I don't suppose any of you are Catholics" and explains about Our Lady.' This passage seems to have found its way, very little changed, into my novel *Excellent Women.*

A lady describing herself as a one-time anonymous freelance broad-caster, who had heard this talk but had probably never read the novels, wrote to Barbara the only condemnatory letter that I have come across. She says, 'Dear Madam, Re Our Lady at Buckfast Abbey. In view of your snide and sneering comments in the talk last week on the Third Programme, please allow me to enclose this short essay from my weekly (Catholic) paper, the Universe.' The newspaper cutting is missing, so I don't know what is was about, but she went on to say, with some justifi-cation, I thought, 'You probably would not report a visit to a Buddhist temple, and sneer at a representation of a Buddha...' and then contin-ues wildly 'You find it all too easy to denigrate the Christian tradition to which this country owes so much – in the presentation of learning; the care of the sick; the education of children in the Grammar Schools the Church founded in the Middle Ages, etc. etc. Do you read Carl Jung? If so, you will know that towards the end of that great man's life he wrote in his great work on the Archetypes – There is no doubt in my mind that the archetype for Western man is – Christ.'

I'm afraid that Barbara's rather tactless 'Catholic junk' and 'black bee-tles' led to this hysterical tirade; she might have given a less contentious example. In fact I thought the Buckfast Abbey notebook description was considerably toned down in *Excellent Women*, where it appears much less offensive.

While there is a lot to be got from the notebooks, it is hard work digging it out. Some of the pages are written in pencil, which is never easy to read, or are otherwise indistinct, so it is hard to decipher even when one is as accustomed to her handwriting as I am.

It is also uncomfortable work. The chairs in the Reading Room are too low for me, especially if I am using a laptop. I once asked for, and received, a couple of cushions, but they were too flat to make much difference. Apparently, Alfred Hackman, a Cataloguer at the Bodleian in the 1840s, had a similar problem, which led to a minor disaster. According to the new *Oxford Dictionary of National Biography*, 'he was accustomed to work sitting on top of a thick volume which, as a result, he forgot to include in the library catalogue.'

The diaries, which form the second section of Barbara's papers, cover the years 1932-1979. The earlier ones are proper journals in which she expresses her feelings about life and literature. When personal relationships were causing her pain or embarrassment, pages have been torn out – presumably destroyed. Until she started her literary notebooks in 1948, the diaries contain a good deal about her work, especially the history of her first attempt at writing *Some Tame Gazelle*, and the early short stories.

Later diaries simply record appointments, though shopping lists and ideas for new clothes and birthday presents often appear at the back. However, useful, and often amusing, snippets are to be found there.

In the early years of the Society, our first chairman, Elizabeth Proud, an actress and producer with BBC Radio, used to select readings from the novels and arrange for them to be read at conferences by well-known English actors, like Miriam Margolyes, Joanna David and Benjamin Whitrow. In 2002 we started a new trend by having members of the Society perform the short story 'The Pilgrimage', which I had already copied from the archives, as a dramatized reading. The following year the theme was anthropology, with reference mainly to *Less Than Angels* – a topic that was dear to my heart, since I had worked at the International African Institute in the early 1960s. I had previously come upon 'Parrot's Eggs', a radio play about a group of social anthropologists which Barbara had submitted to the BBC in 1949, but which had been rejected, and I thought it would fit in very well at this conference. I had to make certain minor changes to both the format and the text to improve presentation, but the play was essentially unchanged. In 2004, under the theme 'Mothers and Other Relatives', I chose for the reading slot 'Mothers & Fathers', a story which had caught my attention early on as being very funny, if a bit macabre. For the background to all these, the notebooks and diaries provided some information, but, particularly for 'Mothers & Fathers', much was also gleaned from the third section of Barbara's archive, Correspondence.

I had thought that 'Mothers & Fathers' was the obvious choice for the September 2004 conference, even without realising, since I had not read any of her books, that it was a parody of the work of Ivy Compton-Burnett. However, the very well-read Hazel Bell immediately recognised the style, and I was then directed by a reference in *A Lot to Ask* to the correspondence between Barbara and Robert Liddell, where I found its full history.

Barbara did not much like *More Women than Men*, the first Ivy Compton-Burnett she had read, but Robert Liddell's enthusiasm made her revise her opinion. They started to write to each other in Compton-Burnett style, using such phrases as 'what could be his meaning' and 'I would not tolerate it'.

In September 1936 Robert wrote 'Let us, as you say, practise C-B style. I shall do a short story in it as an exercise, some time when I have leisure'. Barbara, however, was quicker off the mark with 'Mothers & Fathers', for on 10 November Jock wrote again:

> Thank you for your lovely story – Donald [his brother] and I thought it exceptionally funny – we particularly admire the scene where Henry and Ingrid Godenhjelm enter their new home, and the *full lives* of so many of the characters. I wonder how Miss Ivy Compton-Burnett would enjoy it? Your use of *giving the words their full meaning* is particularly felicitous, also the *burden of sin*, and Donald could not stop laughing over *Denton, we have led wicked lives. Many can call us father.* I am

sorry to say that he has read the first seven pages of my exercise, *More Aunts than Uncles,* without a smile, but it quite amuses me…Is it not easy and delightful to write like that…Don agrees with me that you are the greatest comic writer of the age and every now and then laughs over your story in retrospect. We know much of it by heart. How nice that Henry and Elsie enjoyed it – but do you think Elsie who has not read C-B can possibly appreciate your story? I think she says 'outstanding' because Henry tells her to.

This is, in my experience any way, a rare instance of the accurate dating of a story, and the circumstances leading to its writing. Possibly further reading of the letters may provide more information of this sort. Fortunately, Robert Liddell's handwriting is very clear and easy to read, but not so with all correspondents; Bob Smith, for example, had an almost illegible scrawl!

The Correspondence files are an excellent resource. Some letters Barbara wrote to friends like Robert Liddell and Bob Smith have been donated by the recipients to the library, but other correspondence is of course largely one-way and includes letters of appreciation from friends and strangers alike. I was able to use some of these fan letters, along with reviews from newspapers and magazines, to describe the public reaction to *Some Tame Gazelle* at the 2001 conference.

When *Quartet in Autumn* appeared after so long a silence, one admirer wrote, 'I am so glad that you are not dead. I was so dreadfully sorry when you suddenly stopped writing, and could see no reason other than demise why you should have done so…'

Many readers told her of the difficulties they had in finding her books, especially if they came to read her in the 1960s and 70s when many were out of print. One reader had to 'battle with her conscience' before returning a Pym to the library – she had thought of saying that she had lost it! Others remarked on the superiority of her themes to the general trend: 'Your books are so wholesome, and the people so human, that it's a relief to be able to turn to them when so much rubbish is being churned out.' And 'There are still many of us who do not care for the rather peculiar sexy books now published.' A few wrote, some at tedious length, asking her help in getting their own books published.

Most of these letters were from women, but by no means all. One man described her books as 'balm for the spirit' after his father's death. Another, who had just finished reading *The Sweet Dove Died,* said that he had been working on a freighter, and had read about her in *Time* or *Newsweek* in Manila. A third, in Nairobi, invited her to visit, and another wrote glowingly of her books, and said

> I can add only one more thing which is personal, and that is about your understanding of the position of gay men – and I write as one. The magnificence of chapter 17 of *A Glass of Blessings* makes me gasp at its rightness. [Incidentally, this is the chapter that Penguin Books in the U.S. later asked to include in the *Penguin Book of Gay Fiction.*]

There is some evidence that Barbara answered many of these letters, and was generous with her advice. I wonder how she replied to the lady who wrote, 'May I tell you how much I enjoyed hearing you speak on Radio 3 this evening. Your book, *The Vet's Daughter* [actually written by Barbara Comyns], has always remained in my memory, and I have searched fruitlessly for further work by you throughout the following years.'

Hilary was faced with a similar misunderstanding in 1994 when the editor of an anthology which was to be illustrated with pictures of eminent writers with their cats, asked for 'a photograph of Barbara Pym taken with her cats Links, Dor, Buddye and Poopa in 1938.' [These were in fact family nicknames for Irena, Frederick, Barbara, and Hilary Pym, respectively.]

This last bit, of course, I found among the newly deposited material. A large quantity of papers was given to the library by one of Hilary's legatees after her death. These fill two shelves in a store room opposite the Reading Room, and have yet to be given the treatment by the archivists. I'm afraid it appears that this will not happen very soon, owing to lack of resources. I have looked at some of the papers, going through them in the order in which they are shelved. The first is a hard-backed exercise book, within which are a couple of loose papers. One of these is the poem 'Something to Love' by Thomas Haynes Bayly, written in her own hand, from which Barbara took the title of her first novel.

The other is a photocopy of the cutting from the *Times*, commenting on the famous TLS article, called 'How are the Mighty Fallen – according to the Critics', which Philip Larkin had sent to Barbara in January 1977.

This piece concentrated largely on overrated authors, among whom were Arnold Toynbee, E. M. Forster, André Malraux, Freud and Virginia Woolf. Others to get the thumbs down were, more surprisingly, perhaps, Tolkien, Orwell, Sartre and Wittgenstein, though in fairness it must be said that each of these was nominated by only one critic.

The exercise book itself contains cuttings of reviews of radio talks and books, including reissues of earlier novels. There are among them eleven pages of reviews of *Some Tame Gazelle*, twelve of *Excellent Women*, seven of *Jane and Prudence* and twelve of *Less Than Angels*. (This may explain why I could not find any reviews of *Less Than Angels*, when I talked about that novel in 2003.) At some point Barbara must have decided to keep reviews separately, and as Hilary continued this practice after Barbara's death, they were not passed over to the Bodleian at that time.

Next come a series of large scrapbooks, started by Barbara and continued by Hilary, containing similar material. As each novel was reprinted after Barbara's second coming, as it were, so a scrapbook would be filled with the ensuing comment. The 1978 scrapbook, for example, contains almost exclusively reviews of *The Sweet Dove Died*, which was published that year. The one for 1980 has Barbara's obituaries, and reviews of *A Few Green Leaves*. 1984 is a fat book with reviews of *A Very Private Eye*. A 1984-5 book consists of a record in words and pictures of Hilary and Hazel's tour in the United States. I was really surprised at the number of newspaper and journal articles devoted to Barbara's novels and to the biographies up to, say, 1995.

Thereafter there are fewer – one scrapbook for 1996-2000, and the last one containing material as recent as the Radio 4 play *The Resurrection of Miss Pym*. It was touching to see how assiduously Hilary maintained these scrapbooks right up until her death in 2004.

Then there is a box of letters sent to Hilary after Barbara's death, and a series of folders headed 'Literary – General' and arranged chronologically, mainly of letters received by Hilary, most of them concerning Barbara and her work, from such luminaries as Lord David Cecil, Philip Larkin, Alison Lurie, A. N. Wilson, Patricia Routledge, and Helen Gardner.

In one of the folders is a letter from a researcher, who has read all the short stories, and names those she thinks would be good to publish, and those she considers weak. For what it is worth, her views were almost entirely opposite from mine!

Barbara and her friends seemed to enjoy parodying the works of others. I have already mentioned Barbara's imitations of Tennyson, Pope, and Aldous Huxley, and the Ivy Compton-Burnett skits with Robert Liddell. Robert wrote a poem 'To Cassandra upon her book' after he read the first draft of *Some Tame Gazelle*, and another 'On Mr. B, his voiage into Juttland' when John Barnicot went to visit Henry Harvey in Finland; both are written in mock classical style, with appropriately archaic spellings.

I was pleased to find among these new papers that a younger generation was continuing this practice. Here is an unsigned verse, which Hazel Holt has recently told me was written by her son Tom, parodying the Bard, no less:

Lines on a Bowl of Smarties,
observed at Henry Harvey's cottage at Willersey

Fear no more the midnight sun
Nor the Reindeer's fierce intention
Thou thy worldly task have done
Home art come, and drawn thy pension
Even *jeunesse dorée* must
As Smartie People come to dust.

Fear not Academe's Discord
Nor the frost's insidious bite,

Fear no half cooked smorgasbord
Nor the well-armed Muscovite
For even Henry Harvey must
As Smartie Person come to dust...

No preface writer beard thee
American come near thee
No spiteful critic hurt thee
No footnote disconcert thee
At produce shows receive due praise
And in Riseholme spend thy days.

And another by Tom, this time signed, 'For Hilary at Finstock', a sonnet in imitation of Rupert Brooke. [Ramsden is a village neighbouring Finstock, and presumably considers itself superior.]

Now Ramsden people rarely smile
Being urban, squat and full of guile
But Finstock folk, best folk on earth
Maintain their honest rural worth
In smoky cottages, where Truth
And Justice dwell beneath the roof.

Disdainful Ramsden, though you try
You'll not pass through the needle's eye,
And virtue makes a braver show
Than saunas, Audis, video
And all the trappings of your wealth.
Ah γνῶθι σαυτόν: know thyself;
Stands the quartz clock at ten to three
And are there kous-kous still for tea?

That's about as far as I have got with this new material. I have to stress that this material is very difficult, almost impossible, to use in its present state – one can only browse.

It will be evident to you that my 'research' on Barbara's papers in the Bodleian Library has been somewhat superficial. I have done little systematic searching, and there are large sections that I haven't even looked at. I've merely dipped in here and there as circumstances dictated and time permitted, and I have contributed nothing at all to scholarly debate. Nevertheless, I feel pleased and very privileged to have had the opportunity to look at these papers and to present to our members, through *Green Leaves*, and at conferences, some of Barbara's unpublished work. I am sure that they have enjoyed reading and hearing it as much as I have finding it.

Earlier versions of this paper were presented at the 2005 North American Conference in Cambridge, Massachusetts and the 2008 Annual General Meeting in Oxford.

3

Rupert Gleadow: Barbara's First Oxford Romance

1932 – 1943

15 October 1932. Today I must always
remember I suppose. I went to tea with Rupert
(and ate a pretty colossal one) – and he
with all his charm, eloquence and masculine
wiles, persuaded…

3

Rupert Gleadow: Barbara's First Oxford Romance

Barbara went up to St Hilda's College in October 1931, but we have no record of her first term at Oxford; her diaries in the Bodleian archives begin in January 1932. The first of these is a fat hard-backed exercise book, containing spasmodic entries – Barbara was not a disciplined diarist – up to September 1933. On the first page Barbara has written 'A record of the adventures of the celebrated Barbara M. C. Pym during the year 1932', demonstrating that she was still very much the school-girl.

Although we have no record, it is clear that Barbara made many friends during her first term, at the end of which, incidentally, she failed Pass Moderations, the compulsory examination at the end of a student's first term. As well as Mary Sharp, Dorothy Pedley and Mary Topping at St Hilda's, there were also male students, including Bill Thacker and Teddy, surname unknown, who both wrote to her during the Christmas vacation.

> I'm looking forward awfully to going back but I simply must work hard. A new term in a new year – golden opportunities (and how!) to get a Moderator, a peer's heir, a worthy theological student – or even to change entirely! I'm really thrilled about going back, especially to see my darling Moderator.

Barbara had a crush on one of these Dons who set and mark examination papers, but whose names were not always known to the students. She called him Fat Babyface, and looked out for him whenever she was in town. One afternoon she saw him in the High and tried to shadow him, but she lost the trail.

> Funny what a curious desire I have to see my Fat Babyface, too sweet in spite of other people's unfavourable opinions. Some-

how I'm sure he's Kenneth B. McFarlane of Magdalen. Unfortunately I couldn't judge whether he'd come out of Queen's or Magdalen, so his name still remains rather an uncertainty. Really this is the queerest crush ever – I wonder if he has any inkling.

Later Barbara became disenchanted with him and transferred her admiration to another Moderator.

In *A Lot to Ask*, Hazel Holt says, 'Even before she went to Oxford, Barbara had shown a remarkable propensity to fall in love with people she didn't actually know', and this diary has many such examples. As well as the Moderators, Barbara had her eye on two Scholars at St Edmund Hall, to one of whom she referred as 'the green scholar', presumably from something he had worn; the other she called 'my secret passion from Teddy Hall. He has an interesting face. I'm sure he must be worthwhile.' She also noted that he looked 'very heavenly in plus fours'. Whenever she was returning to St Hilda's she contrived to go via New College Lane and Queen's Lane. Once, just as she was passing Teddy Hall 'someone came out with a bicycle. It was my pet scholar. I traced him up Iffley Road, so it should be quite easy to find his name.' She made notes of her sightings of him, and eventually discovered that he was Geoffrey Walmsley, doing a diploma in theology.

This habit of observing and trailing people was one which she would continue throughout most of her life.

Names of other men that she did know appear in bewildering profusion in her diary. Gary, who is merely named; Bill Thacker, a frequent escort; Harry Harker, who was infatuated with her and later asked her to marry him; Ross: 'He really is angelic and great fun'; Aidan: 'I think he's a bit too curious for my taste'; Wells: 'Sweet, but too intellectual'; Harlorin: 'An amusing creature'; John, in his pink shirt and tie. 'It would amuse me to see him again'; and Teddy, who sent her a letter beginning 'Darling Barbara!' 'Poor man – but I've just got to be firm with him.' Nevertheless she continued to go out with him quite often. Still, she went on collecting:

Went on the river this afternoon. Got to know Leslie Fearnehough (Queens) and Michael Rabone (Univ), because we wanted to borrow a match. I hope they didn't think we were deliberately trying to make a pick-up – really I do some unfortunate things – but how can you smoke a cigarette without a match?

But Barbara did work hard in spite of her hectic social life, turning in essays on time, and enjoying lectures by such notable scholars as Edmund Blunden, J. R. R. Tolkien and C. S. Lewis, and passing her P. Mods at the second attempt.

For the rest of the term, and during the vacation, Barbara concentrated her attention on Geoffrey, and in Trinity term she confided to her diary:

Oh, Geoffrey, how I love you! And I suppose nothing will ever happen about it. And I'll just forget when you go down.

And on 18 June:

I saw Geoffrey for the last time – he had a most beautiful smile on his face when I saw him. Sweetheart, good-bye! 'Auf Wiedersehen my dear.' But even now I can't believe that I've almost certainly seen his dear face for the last time ever!

On that same day Barbara received a letter from Rupert Gleadow, the first of very many. Rupert had come up to Trinity College in 1928 from Winchester, and was working for his final examinations in Classics and Egyptology. He shared rooms with George Steer (Christ Church). His letter confirmed an invitation to tea for

26th May, 4 o'clock, 47 Wellington Square. I haven't yet asked anyone else on Thursday, I hope you don't mind? Did you intend a flattering suggestion when you said you had done no work since you saw me in the Bod? Probably not, but Bill Thacker complains he has not heard of you at all for a number of days! I also have done almost no work but that was partly because I had to arrange our gaudy on Trinity Monday.

Yours till Thursday (and after, I hope). Rupert

Barbara mentioned the occasion in her diary:

Today was an important day. I went to tea with Rupert

Gleadow whom I had formerly met at Bill's in Michaelmas term, and also at a flick with Bill on May 10th. In the Bod on Wednesday 18th he invited me to tea and I accepted, wanting to see more of him. I went at 4 – we had tea in George Steer's sitting room – it was littered with books and we had tea off a table covered with a skin. On his sofa were lovely leopard skins. [The leopard-skinned couch was to play more important parts later.] We ate a large tea and talked much. We got on amazingly well – Rupert was far more human than I thought. It surprised me when he put his hand on mine – and when he asked me to kiss him I was even more amazed, but I refused!

On 28 May 1932 Rupert wrote again:

Dear Barbara

It was so nice having tea with you on Thursday. I suppose the University would not allow me to come and call on you, otherwise they'd have all sorts of Don Juans getting in.

Yesterday every street I came out of I looked carefully round to see if you weren't in sight! Today I am going to look for you in the Bod at 12.45 and 6.30…

Hoping to see you soon, Your Rupert.

And in a second letter later that day:

My dear Barbara

I've been trying to work, but it's no good – no good at all. The Egyptian sage whom I was reading kept on putting [here he gives the Egyptian hieroglyphs for 'Barbara'] in the most ungrammatical places in sentences, and finally…I gave it up.

They met again on the Saturday and spent most of Sunday together:

After spending that whole Sunday morning with you I felt so impressed by my wickedness that I sat down and did almost 5 hours work without stopping; but it needed OH such a lot of strength of mind, I was quite tired afterwards – so that the next morning I had such a nice time lying in bed more than half asleep and dreaming about you.

With all my love, Rupert.

The following Thursday, 2 June 1932, was Barbara's 19th birthday.

> Barbara Darling
>
> It occurs to me that I haven't got you a present yet for your birthday and wouldn't you like to come with me to choose it? And also further that if you aren't going out on Thursday you really ought to, you know, and we might go to *Rookery Nook* or *Frankenstein* (since you've seen *The Constant Nymph* – hope it was good) – and if so I ought to get tickets beforehand.
>
> With all my love, Rupert.

And in yet another letter on Wednesday he said:

> My dearest Barbara,
>
> I am sending this by post just so that it shall reach you first thing tomorrow morning to wish you a very happy birthday, and lots of happy birthdays, and may they all come after one another as slowly as possible, so as to make you stay young and jolly like ever so – and I do hope I meet you again when we're both far older, and hear that it's all come true and that you've had a lovely time always...
>
> Love from your Rupert.

On her birthday Rupert took her to Elliston's and bought her 'a heavenly scarf, royal blue and orange'. They had dinner at Stewart's with Rupert's friend and fellow Egyptologist from Worcester College, Miles McAdam, and then went to see the film *Frankenstein*.

The following day (Friday) Barbara went to tea with him again:

> After much pleading I let him kiss me, though I didn't enjoy it as much as I was to later – at this time I had not forgotten Geoffrey.

On Saturday morning the infatuated Rupert wrote again:

> Barbara Darling,
>
> I just can't face any work just now so I'm writing to you instead...it's a comfort to think we shall meet tomorrow at 10.15. Trevor Wylie saw us walking down the High together yesterday – I just saw him out of the corner of my eye; and

then found a note in my rooms "How are you?" I haven't been able to tell him that the answer is HAPPY … Goodbye darling for the present. Yesterday and you were a marvellous pair, and so will you be tomorrow.

With lots of all my love, Rupert.

On Sunday 5 June they went to Boars Hill:

We went into a wood and sheltered from the showers. He was very Theocritean [pastoral, idyllic] and loving. I got a wee bit sick of it, but tried to please him as I was determined to treat him as kindly as possible as he had Schools [written final exams] on the 9th.

Afterwards he wrote to her:

Barbara Darling

It's been the most marvellous day, and I haven't stopped thinking about you the whole time. Boars Hill really has some very nice uses, particularly in its more obscure glades…but what I'm looking forward to most are those lovely days after term…Darling, my memory is going to take special care of today, and never forget how lovely you have been, and how kind. Goodnight – and now to dream about you.

My love to you always, Rupert

Barbara wrote in her diary on 7 June:

In the evening we had a last do before Schools. Miles came too and it was great fun. Dinner at Stewart's, plus liqueurs, then *The Case of the Frightened Lady* at the Super. I felt sad but happy saying good-bye to Rupert. Sad because I thought I wasn't going to see him for ages, happy because I liked him so much.

Rupert's Schools were from 9 to 14 June, with the viva [oral examination] on the 16th. They did manage one evening together, the three of them, on 13 June, at the Queener to see *Goodnight Vienna*:

We sat at the back in the corner and I had two arms around me for the first time in my history.

After his viva:

> I met Rupert at the corner of the Turl and he told me the joyous news that they'd both got Firsts!

As his mother was to be in Oxford for the weekend, Rupert and Barbara did not meet again until Monday, but from then until the vacation started – only five days – they were inseparable, and usually accompanied by Miles. There was no need for letters during this period, but Barbara noted some of their doings in her diary:

> *20th June.* Rupert and I drank chocolate at the Queener, and went on to no. 47. Oh blessed George Steer and his lovely leopard skins – I hope he gets a First!

He did! After lunch at Elliston's the next day they drove to Ramsden, Great Tew and Charlbury, and back in Oxford drank sherry, ate at Stewart's and went to the Super:

> *22nd June.* We dined at Stewart's and I felt in a very sentimental mood – mainly because the radio played *Auf Wiedersehen*. Then we went to 47 and finished up George Steer's port. We all behaved rather appallingly.

> *23rd.* Rupert and I went to buy some things for lunch as we intended to take it with us on the river. Rupert quoted to me Marvell's 'To His Coy Mistress' and 'Definition of Love' – I had never heard them before. The more one talks with him the more one realises that he really is brilliant. Then on to the river. Getting in to the punt I half fell in, and Miles got his trousers entirely wet trying to rescue me … I rushed back to St Hilda's and changed, then we went to The Spreadeagle at Thame. We ate a marvellous dinner at which everything ordinary, like fish, tasted extremely good.

> *24th June.* Rupert and Miles came and we went off for lunch at Stewart's where they played *Wien du Stadt meiner Träume* – I heard it for the first time there. At the station I held Miles' and Rupert's hands tightly and gazed in to their blue and brown eyes respectively. Then we said good-bye and I settled down to a sober journey home. A marvellous ending to a marvellous term – Geoffrey, Rupert and Miles – everything. My first Trin-

ity term has set a perilously high standard for the others to keep up to.

Just before he left, Rupert had written to her:

> My darling Barbara
>
> If I'd been told five weeks ago how happy we should be three together I should *not* have believed it. I think Miles finds it a great comfort to have our company. I think you don't mind two at once. This I suppose is my last letter to you from Oxford. With lots and lots of love and kisses, Rupert.

They wrote to each other frequently during the long vacation, though whether they would ever meet again now that Rupert had left Oxford was in doubt. His letters are very romantic, recalling the happy days they had spent together. But he is also preoccupied with his future career about which he vacillates endlessly, undecided whether to return to Oxford to do a D.Phil., or whether, because of his interest in flying, to join the Royal Air Force.

On Sunday 26 June 1932, he writes from his mother's flat in Queen's Court, West London, where he says 'I suffer from atrophy of the emotions owing to boredom,' though he has only been there a few days:

> Barbara my darling
>
> I'm alone in the new flat with my mother, and oh, what a change from Oxford. Miles stayed with us two nights, and went to the air display with us.

This is the first we hear of Rupert's interest in flying.

> I can give you as yet no better idea of my plans for next year than before; I may still go into the Air Force.
>
> I rather spend my spare time wondering what parts of that last week I shall remember best: those lovely nakedish times by the Cher, and Miles with his trousers on a paddle, and you upside down; or Charlbury and Great Tew; or Thames; or *Goodnight Vienna*, and certain hours, particularly one Monday, one 21st June, on a leopard-skinned sofa in Wellington Square. 'But what has been is past forgetting'. Also a lovely time in a wood

on Boars Hill. It's all been very marvellous, and for an end to one's last term uniquely and most appropriately charming. Miles and I thought of you a lot while we were together, and wondered whether you were merrily chattering to your family about the events of the last few weeks, or inventing activities to account for the time which really went in flirting...

I have a great deal to thank you for, which I here and now do. I hope we meet again.

With all my love, Your Rupert.

Barbara did not keep up her diary for the first part of the long vacation though she has a general entry for July:

At first I was bored but gradually settled down – letters from Rupert and Miles helped ...but I was always thinking of Geoffrey – there were some days when he was never out of my mind. He got a distinction in his theology diploma – he was the only one who did! On July 9th Rupert sent me *The Weekend Book*, most charmingly inscribed – and a long letter – one of the nicest I've ever had from him.

I have a copy of the first edition of *The Weekend Book*, edited by Francis Meynell and published by his Nonesuch Press in 1924. Rupert had previously written to her:

I have been reading the Great Poems in *The Weekend Book*, particularly the more modern ones, Flecker and Brook and Francis Thompson, and enjoying them a lot, and it occurred to me that possibly your family has been so slack as not to have a copy: in which case I will give you one as perpetuum monumentum Ruperti S. Gleadow BA because it is always useful and amusing. In case you don't know it I subjoin, as they say, a list of contents.

This he does in some detail, illustrating how his long letters were not always confined to the subjects of love and his career.

...the advantage of this kind of book is that you don't just read it and put it away on a shelf and forget about it, but you read it in little bits at all sorts of times afterwards. I have just learned

Vaughn's 'The World' and 'Helen of Kirconnell' out of it – but then I learn poetry so very easily.

As well as being bored, Rupert was concerned about his future, and seemed permanently short of money despite the fact that the family owned a 51-acre estate in Surrey.

On 2 July, Rupert had written from Bakeham House, Englefield Green, the family home in Surrey, which was to be sold later that month. His father had died in 1930, and Rupert had gone there to clear up the house before the auction, and in doing so had 'destroyed hundreds of old letters of my grandparents and their relations, going back to 1839'.

> My Darling Barbara
>
> Thank you for your lovely long letter, and the photographs … the one I am most glad to have is the one of you. Your letter I got on Thursday evening on coming in rather late, and when I got rid of my tiresome family I took it to bed and read it straight through twice … When I am alone, and have got free from the depressing keeping up of appearances that the company of my mother always entails, then I always seem more, and more naturally happy than I used to before; and I think that must be the result of all the happy times we had in Oxford and I do miss you, you know, and I don't envy you a bit at Oswestry if there really are no young men for you to console yourself with. If absence makes the heart much fonder, I shall be in love! Fancy that! … I'll tell you in my next letter why the arguments are so strong that I should go into the Air Force.

Rupert had some problem with his eyesight, and the result of his visit to the oculist might make a difference to his thoughts about flying:

> As the oculist may make all sorts of differences to my thoughts about flying, I'll not write you now about the Air Force… I somehow think the D.Phil. is more probable, though I'm rather afraid of not being able to get thro' the subject in 2 years… Maybe I'll go to Germany instead of Greece, but they do seem to be killing an awful lot of people there these days with street riots and all that.

On 17 July:

> Barbara Darling
>
> …so many things have happened since I last wrote. On Friday July 8 I made up my mind; on Saturday July 9th I bought an aeroplane!!!! Till last Friday I was occupied in getting my licence out of the Air Ministry, and yesterday I flew it myself for the first time. Of course, I am broke henceforward. The machine is very old and 2nd hand, a special Moth with a racing fuselage whereby it goes faster than the ordinary of its kind … and by the way my eyes are much better: I had no difficulty in landing an aeroplane! …I'm still as vague as ever about my plans: yesterday the D.Phil took a turn for the worse … There being no aerodrome anywhere near Oswestry, I suppose I shan't have a chance to take you up at present, but let me know if you go and stay in Liverpool again. I could do it from there…

Rupert vacillates between the Air Force and returning to Oxford, and considers a few other career possibilities:

> Being bored so much in London…makes me think I must be very susceptible to boredom; and, as I'm very much afraid I should be bored in the Air Force, I've more or less decided not to go in to it. Then as far as going in to His Majesty's service in the Levant, that means learning languages for a year, and after that I'm very much afraid there's an examination, which is unthinkable. As for Egyptology, all the intrigues about the Readership at Oxford have shown me what to expect there, and what sort of people academic people are. So that's not very attractive either…I don't want to take up Egyptology professionally, so to come to Oxford and take a D.Phil. for 2 years would be a sheer swank and probably a waste of time. So I've decided probably not to do that – certainly not if I don't get the Derby Scholarship.

The Derby Scholarship was awarded by the University for two years to a candidate of sufficient merit offering a subject connected with the languages and literature of ancient Greece and Rome.

So we have now gone all the way round the circle and come

back to the Air Force, which is the quickest way of getting paid
(one begins at about £350 a year), and where I should have to
amuse myself by writing in my spare time – which would be
plentiful...

And then, another *volte face:*

> Stop Press! I may come to Oxford to learn modern Greek from
> Professor Dawkins concurrently with, or instead of, the
> D.Phil., with a view to becoming a Professor of Modern Greek!
> (a much more humane and less competed-for study than all
> this squabbling Egyptology.)... I think, after my D.Phil. (if
> any) I shall give up being called an Egyptologist...and be called
> a linguist. After all, I ought to know by then Arabic, Greek
> (ancient and modern), German and/or French, Egyptian and
> Coptic, besides Latin and English, possibly some Italian or
> Spanish – preferably the latter...

Rupert wrote frequently in July – constantly complaining of lack of
money. I can only suppose that his mother paid his expenses, for example for the cruise he was to take in August, but did not give him a
generous allowance; perhaps she was not able to do so until Bakeham
House was sold, and there were no takers for it when it was auctioned
in July 1932. His letters to Barbara were often very long, highly romantic, recalling the times they had spent together, and reiterating how nice
and charming she is.

The cruise, from 12-24 August, was aboard the steam yacht *Killarney*,
from Liverpool to the Scottish Fjords. His letters to Barbara contained
vivid descriptions of the hills and islands through which he sailed, as
well as events on board. At the end of the cruise he went to Newport,
Pembrokeshire, with the intention of spending some time walking in
Wales.

Further thoughts on his career prompted him to tell her:

> About three days ago I started learning Arabic – anywhere from
> Algeria to Persia I may want to speak it – but it's so compli-
> cated I can see I shall have to go almost all through the
> grammar before I begin to understand it ... Egyptian was like

that in the early days. I am now definitely going to go in for the Derby Scholarship and so unless something else turns up I shall be in Oxford from the beginning of term until the award is announced. Then if the award is not to me, I shall go away again.

Somewhere along the line Barbara invited him to stay at Morda Lodge. He wrote from Fishguard on 3 September:

I haven't yet made my arrangements for when I leave here, but I am at present expecting not only to be at Oxford on Oct 10 but to try to get to Oswestry about Sept 16.

From the Post Office at Bala on 7 September, as usual his plans are indefinite:

I propose at present to arrive on Thursday 15th. I can't say exactly yet, because it rather depends on the state of the weather around Snowdon when I'm there. From Bala I'll write and let you know what time I propose to arrive ... I've asked Miles to come to the Lakes with me, and if he is able to we shall probably want to start on 20th...

There were no letters, of course, during Rupert's stay in Oswestry, but Barbara takes up the story in her diary:

Sept 15th. Here follows a perfect week which must be recorded and remembered as about the best of my life. On this day Rupert came. I went to meet him at 3.23 wearing a summer frock and a yellow jersey. I was feeling very shy and very excited. I was pleased to find him about 20 times nicer-looking than his photos. We had tea with Hilary and afterwards talked a lot till supper time. After that we went for a walk down Weston Lane and sat down on the edge of a bridge and talked a lot. Our shyness wore off and we came in at 11.10.

Sept 16th. Seeing me run down a hill Rupert gave me the name of Atalanta. We stopped to have some farewell kisses before going to tea at Ack's, [her aunt, her mother's sister, real name Janie, who lived nearby] and enjoyed some moment of rapturous, most ecstatic madness...

18th. Went for a walk up to the Racecourse where we looked at the scenery. On our way down we stopped several times – many romantic kisses.

21st. We talked a lot – or rather Rupert talked and I listened – about his father and Trinity and lots of things. Before we went out he made the suggestion that we should go to bed – we had much fun and a fight over that. We went down Weston Lane and looked at the stars. I said that the happiness one got out of love was worth any unhappiness it might (and generally does) bring. I can't remember what Rupert said but he wasn't so sure about it not having had the experience I suppose.

22nd. I helped Rupert to pack. I would have loved to go to the Lakes with him and Miles. It was seriously rather awful parting from him. We'd had such a heavenly week together. I never imagined it would be so good. I actually wept a bit!

Rupert wrote to her in much the same vein:

My darling I never realized what it was going to be like parting from you. As soon as you were out of sight I very nearly wept … it was awful….I've called Miles 'Darling' several times … and told him I wished he was you, which he didn't take very kindly … Darling, what can a man say in a case like this? 'Thank you for making me fall in love with anyone so charming as you? Or, for making me realize that I have?'… To me Morda Lodge is the centre of a radiating golden star of happiness, and it must always be marked in gold on my mental map.

Many more letters passed between the two while Rupert was in the Lake District – his very loving, hers too by inference.

Because of all the letters that passed between them, it is easy to forget that the actual time they had spent together was very short – only a few days in May and June, and this week in Oswestry.

At Michaelmas Term they returned to Oxford and resumed their friendship, though its nature was beginning to change. Without Barbara's side of the correspondence, it is difficult to know how interested in Rupert she really was. Their acquaintance in Trinity Term was short, if intense, and much of the time they had been a threesome, when they behaved rather like children happily playing in the sunshine. In the vacation that followed Barbara had been thinking more about Geoffrey than Rupert. She was bored in Oswestry, and Rupert was the only one of her friends who had kept in touch, so his visit probably assumed a greater importance than it deserved. For his part, Rupert's letters were becoming more personal, and he was clearly wishing to take their relationship to the next level.

On her first day back she met him at his new digs in 90 St Mary's Road, and later they dined at Stewart's with Miles, who was back in Oxford with a Senior Scholarship to New College. 'A happy reunion' she recorded. 'It was marvellous.' And at the end of the month they were still very attached to one another:

> Just as I was feeling very bored sweet Rupert called for me. We went first to Trinity and walked in the gardens, then to Iffley, and finally we landed at Miles's digs where we had tea. We spent a most happy, peaceful, loving and lovely evening until supper time.

But three days later she was back to her old tricks:

> I think it was on this day that I first saw the charming scholar. He is heftily built, indeed inclined to be fat – features Byronic – hair dark and thick – face interesting. He intrigued me.

The next day she appeared to be abstracted when she met Rupert, perhaps by thoughts of this new interest, who turned out to be a putting and weight blue from Balliol who is never mentioned again:

> Rupert called for me and we went for a long and energetic walk it being such a fine afternoon. We ate at Stewart's, I think, and went back to Rupert's digs – where we had a pleasant time I imagine.

On 13 October Barbara records, 'Met Rupert in a dark suit and white tie – he persuaded me to have lunch at the Randolph with his mother and Edmund... I was of course terrified but my fur coat gave me confidence ... we all adjourned to Fullers for tea with Mrs Macadam and Miles.'

On 6 November, Barbara wrote that she spent a few pleasant hours with

Rupert in his digs but there are no more entries in her diary until the beginning of the following term.

Rupert now had a growing interest in astrology:

> I've just been lent some books on Astrology, which are very interesting, though here and there one of them is absurd ; but on the whole amazingly true; you should read what it says about Gemini people (I'm Gemini, and so to some extent are you). What time of the day were you born? Do let me know next term. I am now in all sorts of astrological and diary-keeping throes. This morning the post brought me some astrological manuscript notes to copy out, which a lady is lending me, and I've been engaged on them most of the day.

It was in November that Rupert heard that he was not to receive the Derby Award:

> They gave no reason for their decision, but it was because they didn't think the subject was classical enough …However, I merely went and saw Prof Griffith to ask him about ancient Egyptian astronomy and astrology in case of doing that for a D.Phil.

However, it appeared that there was a Don who had already adequately covered those subjects.

> Anyway, I shall not be leaving this University just yet. I don't really want to leave Oxford with you here.

During the winter vacation Rupert was at St Albans, flying. He writes from there on 9 December, 'I'm sending the horoscope.' [A horoscope is a diagram of the heavens, showing the positions of the stars and planets at a given place and time.]

> I don't know whether it is really very good, seeing as how it's the first horoscope I ever did. Really, I think your marriage prospects are quite excellent (so are mine! But I will tell you about my wife one day.) I think it's an extremely fine horoscope and I wish you luck with it.

During the vacation, both were taking stock of the situation, though we only have Rupert's letters, which show signs of an increasing emphasis on sex, to go on. At the same time Barbara seems to be, to some extent anyway, distancing herself from his attentions, perhaps regretting some of her earlier confessions to him. He was intent on seducing her next term:

> My intentions are strictly dishonourable. But it's a difficult art, having a mistress, and Oxford is one of the most difficult places to practise it in. Hence, darling, your still lasting immunity…

while she, unwilling to go to such lengths, was trying to distance herself from him. Oscar Wilde said, 'The very essence of romance is uncertainty', and now that she knew Rupert well perhaps his charm was beginning to fade. She encouraged him not to think of her as his exclusive girlfriend. By the end of the vacation he had taken her at her word:

> By the way, darling, you'll be sorry to hear that at last I've stopped wasting my time; at last I've found…someone with whom I can fulfil my promise to you not to be *strictly* faithful; but as I only made the discovery 2 days ago it's only two days kissing I've been able to have – and I did need it… By the way did you see that in America a man was sent to prison for 'from 1 to 3 years' for seduction! I shall have to look out, if ever I go there!

On 17 January 1933, back after the winter vacation, Barbara writes:

> Rupert called in the afternoon and I found myself remarkably glad to see him. We went on to his rooms in Trinity where we indulged in some very pleasant caresses both before and after tea – but I stuck out against having a real necking party. But really he is charming, and I couldn't be cross with him.

I think it was on this same day that Barbara had caught sight of Henry Harvey for the first time. Perhaps that is another reason why she was so coy with Rupert. From this time on her thoughts were increasingly on 'Lorenzo', and she detached herself gradually from her relationship with Rupert.

For some days Barbara did not know the name of 'the pale scholar' whom she kept seeing at lectures and in the Bodleian, and whom she thought of as 'Lorenzo.' Soon she was writing 'This diary seems to be going to turn into the Saga of Lorenzo'. Certainly Rupert appears in it less and less frequently.

Rupert is as uncertain as ever about his future:

> The mere mention of your rather vicious collections next term made me feel all hollow about my own damn thesis, which I ought never to have started at all. I'm feeling rather tired through lying awake half the night thinking out my future. It's no good. I've got to go down. There's no point in staying on fatuously up here and taking a fatuous D.Phil. I'm too old for the entrance to the consular and other services, but I'm not too old for the diplomatic and foreign office, and I'm damned if I see why I shouldn't try to go into that if there's an examination next August. I ought to be able to learn lots of French and German before then.

And he added, prophetically as it turned out, 'No doubt in the end I shall find Astrology is the only profession left.'

On 23 February 1933 Rupert wrote to Barbara asking her to lunch, and saying, 'After inspecting Harvey, Miles and I decided that various other people look like that – in other words, the face did not seem altogether strange. Well, well!'

So Barbara must have told him of her interest in Henry. In March she went to 'a delightful lunch party at Trinity', which included Rupert, of course, and she saw him again in his digs on 22 April.

But on 29 April Barbara wrote in her diary, 'Oh, ever to be remembered day! Lorenzo spoke to me!' Some days later Henry took her on their first date to dinner at the Trout, where he told her his name was Gabriel. On the following Sunday 'Rupert came to see me in the morning, but I couldn't possibly kiss him because the last mouth to touch mine had been Gabriel's.'

Rupert had finally to accept that Barbara was not for him. As Hazel says in *A Lot to Ask*, 'He tactfully made a comfortable joke of the whole affair', and he bowed to the inevitable with good grace. They continued to correspond and remained friends throughout their time at Oxford, and beyond, though perhaps there was a touch of bitterness in one letter where he suggests that this is what Barbara would say of him in the future:

> There was that poor dear Rupert Gleadow – quite *mad* about me he was, but my dear he really was terribly *trying*, so *lascivious* – never would leave me alone! What did I like him for? Oh, I don't know, I suppose he was rather pathetic – of course an awful poseur – he would make you think he was acutely miserable when all the time the man was devoured by a positive *flame* of sexual excitement. It was most indecent.

On 29 March 1933 he wrote from his mother's flat in Queen's Court, London:

> I am going to take a ticket in the next 2 or 3 Irish Sweeps for astrological reasons. I will, as I said, do your fiancé's horoscope, but NOT of course until you are engaged to someone, and for any one else my fee is now 1 guinea...

By 20 April 1933 there is no doubt at all that the romance was over. In his last letter to her from Oxford Rupert wrote:

> Barbara dearest,
>
> Who have you fallen in love with this time? ...I have not led an entirely unsexual vac, have you? I hope and think perhaps you'd have written if you had...I have got myself all mixed up in Astrology again with several people expecting horoscopes and all my aunts panting for golden prophecies of their futures.

That is the last of the letters from Oxford. Rupert obviously completed the academic year; but I don't think he went back again in October 1933.

Eighteen months later, in October 1934, Rupert wrote from London NW3 asking Barbara about her exam results, which of course she had had the previous June, and tells her:

> You'll be surprised to hear that I have taken up music and am energetically studying the laws of harmony, such of them as are

left in these days. But the writing still continues and I am now settled on Primrose Hill trying to finish a novel by the end of the year. After that I shall probably go abroad again...

No, I am not married, nor anything like it. I think it would be surprising if I were, seeing what my views on the subject are. But at the moment my heart is fairly free. I had a couple of love affairs early in the year, neither very satisfactory. How is your own heart? Pining, I suppose, for some beautiful man, as usual.

Yours ever, Rupert

The correspondence between Barbara Pym and Rupert Gleadow continued after they both left Oxford. Late in October 1934 he wrote:

It was very nice to get your letter, particularly coming so soon. I was sure you'd reply at once, which none of my other friends ever do...Don't you find it an awful strain, writing a novel? I do. However, I've written about 70,000 words already, so it's getting on. I can't tell you what it's all about, it's too strange and mixed. Probably some people will find it shocking but it's not intended to be; only, my hero and heroine show the most awful tendency to go to bed together every time they meet! *I* can't help it, can I?... Very glad to hear that things are going so well with you; surely you must be unique in being able brazenly to say 'No!' when people ask you if you are looking for a job?

Barbara had been twice to Germany in 1934, and had obviously told Rupert about Friedbert Gluck, whom she had first met in Cologne at Easter that year:

It's good that you have been to Germany and can talk about it. Oh, but please don't admire those *filthy* Nazis in their beautiful uniforms: you won't get a chance much longer, because 1936 will just about see the end of Hitler... I suppose you are still as chaste as ever? I'm rather lonely just now, not having had a mistress since the Spring ... Yes, I shall always remember that lovely summer of ours, which was so fine... This morning when I was in my bath the wireless played *Goodnight, Vienna!* I wonder how long we shall go on being able to hear that. It always pleases me. There is also *Wien du Stadt meiner Träume* which was also a theme of that summer.

Will it surprise you to know that I've still got the complete collection of your love letters? A month or two ago I began reading them through, to see if I shouldn't reduce the number, and save space, but I only got half way and so there they are still. They seemed to me to have stood the test of time very well. Mine on the other hand were a little shocking occasionally and I feel they might well be destroyed! You know the saying: 'Do right and fear no man; don't write and fear no women!' However, I shall have to trust you. Best wishes to you and love from Rupert.

Ten months later his next letter was written from the Sesame Imperial Club in London, clearly in response to one from Barbara:

Yes, the Astrology still flourishes; in fact I can answer any reasonably serious question, and collect horoscopes on all sides. My stay in Paris this time has yielded 2 dozen, including Nijinsky and Toscanini and D'Annuncio. Also I have met the best astrologers in England, and in fact have been getting on the 'inside' of that profession. But that is not my real job. My real job – which I could see written in my horoscope and tried to avoid – is political. The principle is this: in lots of countries valuable goods are being destroyed and yet there are people starving. This is unnecessary because we know there is enough to go round. The only thing needful is to distribute it. No orthodox party has any solution for the problem, in fact the only known solution so far is Social Credit – and we have started an ingenious electoral campaign which is already producing results. People will tell you it won't work, but how do they know? And how can they pretend the present system works when food people need is thrown into the sea to keep up prices? However, you won't want a sermon on politics. Only that is the cause I am working for, and in the present state of the world it seems a pretty desperate one. We need to work hard, but we shall get there.

Social Credit was a political theory originated by a Scot, Major Clifford

Hugh Douglas (1879-1952), which argued that 'economic reform would prevent the destruction of soils and food for the sake of profit and ensure that the whole population would be guaranteed sufficient income to enable them to buy fresh, protective foods.'[1]

> Mother is still at Queen's Court... Since going round South America she's been to Baghdad and is now seriously trying to get married again. From her horoscope it looks as though she might succeed and regret it.
>
> As for my novel, well I wrote two and didn't like either of them. They were too much the distillation of the superfluous bile of a thoroughly discontented person. That's because I was not working hard enough and was trying to evade my miserable destiny...and my sex life was unsatisfactory. I wrote a number of short stories too, and some of them I did try to publish, but the form did not come easy to me. They were too strained, and so naturally they didn't succeed. Short stories being a technique nowadays rather than an art, it is easy to get too self-conscious about them...
>
> No, I'm not married... As for you, I know you'll marry all right, though not for a year or two, and to a very nice and rather original man. The horoscope is at home, and I remember most of it – Mars in Aries, Moon and Venus in Taurus, Sun, Mercury and Saturn in Gemini, Ascendant 2 degrees Leo, and Uranus very strong in the House of Marriage.
>
> I'm afraid I never realized your attraction for Henry Harvey was really so serious as to be still among the emotional possibilities. I always imagined him a rather *painted* god, not real. However, he seems to have made an impression on a poor maiden heart.

And, again, obviously in reply to a question from her:

> Yes it is possible to love more than one person, perhaps more than two, for that is the case with me at the moment. I will admit, after your own candour [this will be when she told him that she was in love with both Henry and Friedbert], that I have one mistress in France, and another in Russia, and what should be a third in England. The only thing is that in a case

like that one is always conscious that it is the other person who loves best, for one cannot give one's own heart to more than one person. And it is rarely enough that one can give it to one. And of course one cannot, under any circumstances love a real Nazi....

Yes, no doubt we have changed. This letter will tell you a good deal for it is written quite spontaneously and very fast...but I don't think any of it will surprise you, either on the sexual or political plane. Your own sounded, as you suggest, a bit colder and more disillusioned, but I am sure that you only find it a bit hard to write really naturally, because it is such a long time that is due to the conjunction of Saturn and the Sun... Do you remember George Steer [he of the leopard skin sofa!], who was in digs with me in Wellington Square, but lent me his room to have you to tea in once or twice? He is now *The Times* Special Correspondent in Addis Ababa, so if you read about Abyssinia in *The Times*, it's him.

I'm beginning to realize that one day it will be convenient to be married and have a woman to look after me, but at present I still feel very much the wanderer – 1934 I had the misfortune to spend all in England, with three unsuccessful love affairs, so I was very glad, when Christmas came, to flee to Munich – and now I'm devoured by the desire to see Hungary and the Balkans... I took the M.A. in June, Miles is finishing his D.Phil. and will take his degree in October and after that he is going out to excavate in Nubia for the winter.

The next communication is a postcard from Bregenz, postmarked 25 August 1935:

After an idyllic month in the north Tirol at 3000 ft...I go to Dusseldorf to represent England (probably not officially) at the International Astrological Congress, and am continuing to write two books in the time.

At the end of August, when Barbara was in Budapest she received another postcard from Rupert suggesting that she visit him in London on her way back. 'I'd love 2CU,' he says, using the abbreviation for 'to see you' that kids today use when texting. But Barbara apparently did not take up the invitation, for Rupert wrote in October:

> I had hoped that you would reply to my letter inviting you to
> see me in London…but since you did not I am full of curiosity
> to know whether it was because you thought your reply would
> not arrive in time…or because after the confessions in my letter
> you felt it would not be safe!… As an astrologer, I feel now ex-
> empted from the effort of writing further novels. I have
> discovered the political cause that is going to make most head-
> way and propose to devote my energies to it – viz. Social
> Credit. Why don't you start a group in Oswestry? Or order it
> [the newsletter, presumably], tuppence weekly, from your
> newsagent. As we are going to win our battle I'm naturally keen
> to do so as quickly as possible and get it over, after which I shall
> retire under a pseudonym to Cornwall and predict disasters for
> the Sunday Dispatch. Perhaps!… Yours politically and pertina-
> ciously, if somewhat intermittently, and with love, Rupert.

Late in October he writes:

> Thanks so much for your great letter complete with photo-
> graph: I think you look fiendishly intelligent but very
> agreeable… Your account of Budapest was very intriguing… I
> think I may go there for a Xmas holiday.

The next item in the archives is a newspaper cutting with a surprising
announcement:

> The marriage will take place on December 7th, in Paris, be-
> tween Rupert Seeley Gleadow of 6 rue de Belloy, Paris 16e, son
> of the late Frank Gleadow of Bakeham House, Englefield
> Green, Surrey, and of Mrs. Harold Bompas of Flat 10, 24 Pal-
> ace Court, London W2, and Mlle. Marguérite Rendu,
> daughter of the late Eugène Rendu and of Mme. Rendu of
> Paris.

So Mrs Gleadow did marry again. There is a Harold Bompas who donated a sculpture in 1937 and three paintings in 1941 to the
Ashmolean Museum; perhaps this was Rupert's step-father. And there
was a Marguérite Rendu who translated detective fiction from English
into French between 1930 and 1937 who could have been his fiancée.

The provenance of this cutting is uncertain, but in the light of later communication I think the wedding date must have been December 1937.

After the newspaper cutting is a letter from Palace Court, dated 5 December 1938:

Dear Barbara

I had intended to write to you long ago for I did not think you could have seen the announcement in *The Times* at the beginning of August. But I've been full of work and terribly weak in health. I shall be here until January 2nd and if you like to see me you have only to ring up or drop a line.

One learns to love, you know, and I began learning in 1932. It seems incredible to realize that in those lovely days none of the tragedies of life had yet happened. But if we had not had those wonderful times together probably I should not have known those sublime heights of love which Marguérite and I together achieved and which will always remain a light to my life.

So you see you have made a difference to my life which I shall not forget. With love, Rupert."

Sadly, I think the announcement in August must have been of Marguérite's death. Rupert's first book, *Astrology in Everyday Life*, published in 1940, was dedicated 'in memory of Marguérite…'

Then, almost another year later there is a letter from Bettiscombe by Bridport in Dorset, a few weeks after the outbreak of war:

Dear Barbara

It is a long time since you heard from me, but for some reason that interval is now at an end – I thought you might like to see the enclosed. [There is no enclosure in the Archive.]

The last year has naturally been pretty unpleasant for me, but I am now staying with some people who are very nice and are willing to bring up my daughter with their own children, so it looks as though that problem were solved. At present she is in France with my old mother-in-law.

This is our first inkling that he had a child. Probably the missing enclosure was a newspaper cutting, or some other evidence of the death of his wife, possibly in childbirth:

> When war began I was near St Tropez having a lovely holiday with sea bathing... The journey back across France in mid-September took a very long time... How are your literary ventures going? I've just written a novel which Raymond Savage [a well-known literary and theatrical agent, biographer of Lord Allenby and the desert campaign of 1922, and advisor on the film *Lawrence of Arabia*] has agreed to handle... I heard about six months ago that Miles was hoping to get married in September... I have no intention of doing any war work until forced to; it is a waste of time for an intelligent person. Hitler is doomed anyway... I hope there are still 57 pubs in Oswestry and that you are in love with some beautiful person as usual. With love, Rupert.

From Bettiscombe, dated 20 January 1940:

> My dear Barbara
>
> Your letter of 8th Dec was a very nice one... You are quite right about my daughter having large black eyes, but in other ways she takes after the mother, being fair, fearless and fond of animals. She was christened Sylvia Marguérite.

It is very sad that we hear no more of Sylvia – whether she ever got back to England before the Germans occupied Paris, or whether the Dorset family took her in. There is no evidence that her father took her back after his second marriage.

> It is impossible to describe my book so you will have to wait till you read it. I am also writing poetry, though with a complete disregard of the modern movement.
>
> Miles got married on Sept 2nd, thinking it best not to give the war a chance to separate them. I saw him the other day on a flying visit to Oxford, but not her, as three months of connubial bliss with so vast a man (he weighs about 14 or 15 stone!!) had necessitated an operation below the belt somewhere, and she was in the Radcliffe. He reported that Tom Thacker is now

Reader in Semitics at Durham and engaged to a very nice girl –
Tom's horoscope suggested marriage to a widow with children!!
Miles has a flat in Oakthorpe Mansions on the Banbury Rd
and is still after 4 years working on the publication of the dig-
gings at Kawa.

I am really very happy here, for I don't think I told you that a
few months ago I met a painter named Helen and we were
both utterly taken with each other at first sight and still are. It
is hard to believe that anyone who loved so well as I did can
begin again, but strange to say it has happened. We suit each
other to perfection, and after living together in the south of
France we are now doing it here… She is a beautiful blonde…
I think we bring it off so well because we are both experienced
and interested in human relationships. Our days are as blissful
as our nights.

With love, Rupert

The last Gleadow entry in the Archive is the horoscope he drew of Barbara some years before, to which he added, 'This being the first
horoscope I ever did is rather liable to contain a few mistakes or inaccu-
racies. RSG'.

Although there are no more letters among Barbara's papers, more must
have been exchanged. She records in her diary on 24 July 1941:

Had a lovely letter from Rupert Gleadow and a copy of his new
book *Magic and Divination.* How lovely it is to be remembered
by one's friends.

Letters must also have passed between them to arrange the visit Barbara
paid to the Gleadows in April 1943, shortly before she went in to the
WRNS, after which she wrote ,'I really feel it did me good going away
and being with Rupert and Helen, who are so blissfully happy together
they hardly seem to be real.'

Apart from her noting his death in 1974, I could find no other mention
of him among Barbara's papers.

One last thought: a far as predictive astrology goes, whether it was Barbara's marriage prospects, the early downfall of Hitler, the fate of the Social Credit party, or the outcome of the 1952 US Presidential Election, Rupert got it spectacularly wrong!

An earlier version of this paper was presented at the 2010 Annual General Meeting in Oxford.

4

Barbara Pym in Germany

1934 – 1938

I was as near to being intoxicated as I've ever been
and was gloriously happy, madly so, with
Friedbert very close to me and his arm around me.
Once he kissed me and I suppose we
didn't behave well – but what did it matter?

4

Barbara Pym in Germany

The story of Barbara Pym in Germany is essentially the story of Barbara and Friedbert Gluck. Hazel Holt and Hilary Walton have given an account of the five visits Barbara made to Germany between 1934 and 1938, and of her relationship with Friedbert, in *A Very Private Eye* and *A Lot to Ask*. I will attempt to draw together the previously published details of this story and enhance them with some of Barbara's diary entries, many of which have never before been revealed.

Why Barbara became interested in Germany in her student days is not clear, but I think that in 1930s England there was considerable interest in, and some admiration for, the country whose economic recovery was demonstrating the power of united national effort; others, of course, were more percipient, like Stephen Spender, who, in his *The Destructive Element,* foresaw the eventual disastrous effect this power would exert over the rest of Europe. There was cultural interest too, in novels like Christopher Isherwood's *Mr Norris Changes Trains* and *Goodbye to Berlin* (though these were both published after Barbara's earliest visit); in the films of von Sternberg and Fritz Lang; and in the popular music of Austria and Germany, which was prominent in the repertoire of Palm Court orchestras and radio programmes in Britain.

Political events did not much interest her at this time, but Barbara loved the music, and was affected by its sentimentality and nostalgia. While on a date with Rupert Gleadow on 22 January 1932 Barbara wrote, 'We dined at Stewarts (upstairs) and I felt in a very sentimental sad mood – mainly because the radio played *Auf Wiedersehen*', and again on 24 June, 'We went off to lunch – choosing Stewarts because of its happy memories and convenience...[There] they played *Wien du Stadt meiner Träume* – I heard it for the first time.'

She was a great picturegoer, as we know, and certainly liked many German films, including propaganda – not, however, *The Blue Angel* which she saw with Harry Harker in January 1932. 'It's a horrid depressing flick, and Marlene Dietrich revolting – but it was interesting.'

We know also that early in 1934 Barbara was frustrated by the lack of progress in her relationship with Henry Harvey, who was being particularly unkind to her, and she longed for a change of scene away from him, temporarily anyway.

Whatever it was that sparked off her interest, in October 1933 Barbara was attending classes in German, a language which she loved and came to study seriously; possibly this was in preparation for a National Union of Students visit to Cologne the following Easter. The NUS web site states that, 'The National Union of Students was established in Britain in 1922 by ex-service people largely as a result of revulsion against the first world war, with an aim to promote world peace and understanding, and to enable British students to be properly represented in the international student body, the *Confédération Internationale des Etudiants*. It soon established a Travel Department which was held in high esteem by the members and actively used.' Unfortunately I couldn't find any details about those early trips.

Her passport and tickets arrived in March 1934, and on Thursday 29 she wrote:

> Today was the beginning of a very happy month in my life which may make some difference to my future…I set off for London…went from Paddington to Trafalgar Square by tube, [then to] the Strand Palace Hotel, where Pedley was waiting.

This was Dorothy Pedley who also went up to St Hilda's in 1931, to read physiology. I think she is one of the girls walking down the High with Barbara in the photograph in *A Very Private Eye*.

> We had some food at a big Lyons Corner House. I don't like them, they are too big, but the food isn't bad and *one can observe life from there*. I remember feeling rather depressed at the thought of Germany.

The italics are mine. This is probably the earliest reference to a lifelong habit that led to many memorable characters in later novels.

Easter was early that year. On Good Friday, 30 March, Barbara and Pedley had breakfast early and walked to Victoria Station through St James's Park. Rather a long walk, I should have thought, especially carrying a suitcase!

> In the train we met a charming Polish girl with red hair and brown eyes, but the other people were quite dull. Then Dover, and arrival at the boat. We had a lovely crossing and never felt the least bit ill. In fact we ate ham sandwiches and chocolate cheerfully – although the prices were scandalous. Ostend proved to be large and clean. We got there about 3.30 and went through the customs, which was far less of a business than I thought it would be. Then into a train and I was surprised to see hard wooden seats for 3rd Class which we were travelling. We got to Brussels soon after 6 and went to dinner. I felt depressed…and almost wished myself back in England. (How little we know of the future.) At 11 o/c our train left…it was lovely gliding into Liège in the early morning. I began to get really excited then. But the most thrilling moment of all was when we got to Aachen, the frontier, and the Customs people came in speaking in German. I managed to talk a little German to a man who came round to look at books [subversive literature?].
>
> Soon after that we were in Cologne – at about 6 o/c in the morning to be exact. I felt very tired and I've never been (and looked) so dirty in all my life! German students met us at the station and there I first saw Hanns Woischnik…Buses were waiting for us at the Station and I staggered in half asleep. We drove a long way to the *Kamaradschafthaus* – where we were to be put up. On arrival we had breakfast – ham and rolls and lots of tea…Then all I wanted was to go to bed…There was a large room with six beds in it arranged in three lots one on top of the other, which Pedley and I shared with two quite dull people. I slept until lunchtime, and even then I doubted whether I was really going to enjoy myself…Then I had my first sight of real Nazis and of Friedbert Gluck. He was wearing black uniform

[of the *Schützstaffel*, or SS, originally formed as Hitler's personal bodyguard but later greatly enlarged], although the others were in yellowish brown shirts with the Nazi swastika business on their left arms. [These would have been members of the *Sturmabteilung*, or SA, Ernst Röhm's private army, many of whom Hitler ordered to be killed in the Night of the Long Knives, the rest being absorbed with the SS under Himmler.]

They saluted each other in the Heil Hitler manner. Then we went into lunch and various speeches were made. Friedbert spoke in German – I remember being much impressed by him, and thinking him a marvellous unapproachable Nazi. What did he look like? Tall, with a lovely figure set off to advantage by the black uniform – very dark with smooth black hair and a high forehead – dark complexion and greyish green eyes, rather strange looking but undoubtedly fascinating. After lunch we went into the town and to the Museum where we went around in parties conducted by German students – we were with a charming boy who spoke English well...The Cologne Museum has some wonderful pictures in it. I was particularly impressed by the huge Rubens pictures and some of the Cologne painters' work of about the 13th century – lovely colour and some wonderful demons in 'The Temptation of St Anthony.' They also had some modern ones – several by Van Gogh – including the well known one of the bridge – an interesting one by Picasso.

After the Museum we went all round Cologne in the buses and saw quite a lot of it. They have some modern looking buildings of which they seem very proud. The cathedral is the centre of the town...and all along one side of the Rhine...Before dinner Pedley and I ventured to the shops and managed to buy cigarettes, oranges, and Pond's vanishing cream, asking for them all in my uncertain German...I can't remember much else of that day, but I suppose I ended up by being still in love with Gabriel [one of Barbara's names for Henry Harvey], however much the Nazis had impressed me.

Sunday 1st Apr: April Fool's Day and the beginning of a new month and I almost think a new period in my life. Today I was completely unfaithful to Gabriel – I mean in the sense I regard it – kissing other people. I began it with a kind of desperation but how it ended is a different story, to be told in good time if I ever finish writing up the account of the next two days.

After breakfast that day Barbara had her first cigarette in six weeks [apparently she gave up smoking during Lent], and then went to the cathedral: 'The Service was Roman Catholic and I could not of course follow it, but the singing was remarkably good.' Then there was reception in the Town Hall: 'I got into conversation with a bearded man of our party who seemed to have taken something of a fancy to me. The afternoon was spent wandering in town and we were shown round by a student – a nice serious young man.' Dinner was at 5, then they went to the opera at 6, where Barbara shared a box with Pedley, the student who had shown them round the town, and another girl:

Die Valkÿrie – very good especially scenic effects, but of course Sigmund was too fat…During the interval I had some beer with Noel Wallace, the bearded man, who seemed quite nice. I went and smoked a cigarette with him, and Friedbert Gluck came and spoke to us. After the 2nd Act I was talking to three nice medical students from London and Friedbert, who translated some of the German summary of the opera for me, in very sweet and not very good English…I had another cigarette with the bearded man and went into his box where he sat on the floor by me and stroked my arm and ankle…after the opera was over I went out with him…we went to the Café Wien and had some lovely cool hock…there was a lovely band which played 1933 tangos and Viennese waltzes…the man is doing research in psychology at London, he told me. We got to the river and then went to another café – a lower class one – where there was real dancing and fat families swaying in time to the music. We danced too, and I enjoyed it. Then by the river again where he kissed me…

The top half of the next page has been cut out. The lower half continues:

Eventually, about 2 o/c, we got on a train and arrived back at Mulheim, to find others also returning. One of the Germans, Hanns Woischnik, was coming downstairs with a bottle of something so we all went up to somebody's room and had a little party. We made much noise and drank quite a lot. Hanns was a little tight. After the party had broken up Hanns and I went round the corner and he kissed me several times in the German way, perhaps 'with inside lip', but I did not mind. He was very sweet and asked me to go to his...

and the next lines are lost on the other side of the torn-out page. Was Barbara trying to conceal her activities with the bearded man or with Hanns? Both, probably!

Monday 2nd Apr: A day of unmixed happiness – undoubtedly the loveliest of this year. The weather was lovely and we set off for our trip on the Rhine. At first I sat quietly on board the steamer and talked to Pedley, the bearded man and the beautiful Yolande Rolla who had reddish blonde hair and brown eyes. As we were given our tickets for the steamer Hanns looked at me intimately with his bright eyes and said 'How are you?' I was wearing his grey silk scarf with my green frock and little black coat. The Rhine was lovely and full of people canoeing in summer frocks and bathing costumes. We were all happy and waved to each other... After a time I got into conversation with Friedbert Gluck. He was looking sweet and he hadn't shaved because his chin was gloriously black and rough. He was wearing flannel bags and a brown tweed coat – a lovely greenish pullover with a nice flowery sort of tie and exquisite shirt. To crown all a very *schön* green hat. We talked a lot and I tried to practise some German on him. He is fond of sports and is good at skiing. I talked also to Hanns who gave me his address and said I must write.

Friedbert and I moved over to where the sun was. I hardly thought of anything, I was too gloriously happy. Then there was a glorious drinking party with lots of white wine. Fancy being nearly drunk in the morning! I sat by Hanns. We landed at Bonn and went ashore – we were to have lunch there and see the University. I talked to the medical students, one of whom cut off a lock of my hair with a penknife, when we were looking at a chapel! Friedbert and Hanns were of course walking with the officials of Bonn University. After a good deal of wandering we had lunch – a good lunch too, although I felt excited and hot and couldn't eat much. During the many German and English speeches I caught Friedbert's eye and we smiled at each other. It was a merry meal but we had to hurry quickly on board the steamer again to go on to Königswinter. Here I was with Friedbert all the time. He and I with Adelmann led the party to Petersberg. The district is lovely – mountains with forests topping them and romantic looking castles. Many cafes and tables outside of course…everyone happy and lovely weather. We went up Petersberg in a mountain train and in parts it was very steep…woods on each side and lovely air when we got to the top. Arrived at the top we went to a café. It was very hot and sometimes I wore Friedbert's hat to shade my eyes from the sun. The cakes were of a size and lusciousness quite unequalled in England…

After tea we wandered and looked at the lovely view – mountains and woods in the distance – the Rhine and town down in the valley. All the time Friedbert was very sweet – why couldn't I have stayed there always – so happy with someone so nice? At about 6 o/c we went down in the train again, and on arriving in Königswinter we found we had some time to spare, so we went to a café – a lot of us – and had a drink called bohle – or something that sounds like that! It was made with five bottles of wine, slices of orange and various herbs, and stirred round. I cut the oranges and Friedbert did most of the stirring although we all had a turn at it. It was a lovely drink. I walked back to the landing place with Friedbert, and we said how lovely it would be if I could stay, and if we could go together all round this lovely country. It was as romantic as anything could possibly be. Friedbert said he laughed when everything was *too* romantic. We then met the others and saw Hanns again. He paid me charming compliments and said that his afternoon would have been much nicer if I'd been there – and we were all crowded together and he held my hand.

Aboard the steamer again I was with Friedbert and we had a party with some other people. By the time we'd finished there were nine bottles on the table – all empty. I was as near to being intoxicated as I've ever been and was gloriously happy, madly so, with Friedbert very close to me and his arm around

me. Once he kissed me and I suppose we didn't behave well -
but what did it matter. Indeed what did anything matter? We
exchanged addresses… there was much merriment – shouting
and singing too, English and German songs. We sang *God Save
the King* and *Deutschland über Alles*. That rather worried Friedbert although I couldn't understand why. He and Hanns had an
animated talk about it in German. Hanns was drunk I think
but very sweet. Then Friedbert and I went down to the lower
deck and stood in the front of the ship away from the crowd.
'Closed kissed' we stood and watched the lights of Cologne
drawing gradually nearer and it meant saying goodbye I knew,
but somehow I could not care. I was really living in the present
– an exhilarating sensation too seldom enjoyed. It was so lovely
to have someone saying nice things to me after Gabriel's rude-
ness and unkindness. I at last began to realize that there could
be something in my life beyond Gabriel.

Friedbert said he had noticed me before he knew my name and
that I was like the English song, his *Secret Passion*. I feel somehow that even if we never meet again there will always be this
short happiness to remember. Parting seemed at that moment
to be romantic. I sat by him in the bus, and at supper in the
exalted place. I ate very little and gave Hanns' scarf back to
him. Friedbert made a wonderful and passionate speech in
German – which Müller translated, badly Friedbert said. Going
to the Station we stood together in the back of the bus and he
put his arm around me. When we got to the Station we found
that the train didn't leave until 1o/c. Friedbert took my luggage
and found me a place. He kissed me goodbye and we shook
hands publicly. As the train slid out of the station I realized that
I had left my heart behind in Cologne.

Tuesday 3rd Apr: Days were really merged into each other at
this time. I was in a carriage with uncongenial companions,
separated from Pedley, and felt unhappy. Hanns was travelling
as far as the next station…but I couldn't see him to say goodbye which saddened me even more.

The journey home included an overnight stop in Bruges which Barbara
seemed to enjoy in spite of her heartache. Before the English party

broke up the leader suggested that people should write to thank Gluck if they felt they wanted to thank someone. So presumably Friedbert was the main organiser at the Cologne end:

> *Back in London on Thurs 5th Apr:* I wandered among the book-shops in Charing Cross Road and bought Vernon Bartlett's new book *Nazi Germany.* Getting home, I realized all the time I was thinking about Friedbert Gluck and not about Gabriel – at least not with the intensity and longing which had formerly characterised my attitude towards him. I looked quite lovingly over my Cologne souvenirs.

> *Fri 6th Apr – Tues 10th April:* I may as well write up these few days together as there isn't anything special to say about them. One important thing seemed to have happened to me though. My tour in Germany meant that I began to take an interest in Hitler, Nazis and German politics. I made a scarlet box with a swastika on it. I bought a small swastika to wear on a pin. I wrote to Hanns and Friedbert, although I realized that one cannot bring back the past. The prospect of going back to Oxford and the possibility of seeing Gabriel did not really thrill me. The first night I came home we turned on dance music and the programme provided two appropriate tunes. *Let there be no more heartaches, no more tears,* was the first, and as far as Gabriel is concerned I don't think there *will* be any more, but of course I realize that I'm bound to be still fond of him, and I shan't really know how things stand until I see him again. The second tune was the old one *I'll see you in my dreams* – and that is probably the only time I shall see Friedbert again. I thought also of the lovely waltz from *Bittersweet* –

> > I'll see you again
> > Whenever Spring breaks through again –
> > Time may lie heavy between
> > But what has been
> > Is past forgetting.

Here there is evidence that a double page has been removed, in spite of the fact that Barbara said there was nothing special to record. After that intensely romantic episode, Barbara returned to Oxford to prepare for

Schools, as the BA examinations in Oxford were called:

> *Tues 17th April:* The post came and brought me (Oh, joy!) something from Friedbert. A long letter all in German – which I have not yet deciphered, and a lovely snap of him. Also a book containing a speech of Hitler's (in English). Dear Friedbert...I am longing to decipher my letter. I'll do it on the nice large pages of Henry's notebook – it seems a suitable place for such an undertaking.

> *Wed 18th April:* At about 6.30 Gabriel passed by and invited himself in – we talked, and he asked me to supper that evening – very nice it was too – and I felt happy and excited. Henry, by the way, had insisted on reading some of Friedbert's letter [she must have showed it to him, possibly to make him jealous] and had translated a little of it – very satisfactorily. He'd wanted me to bring it to supper that night, but I didn't, although I'd said I would.

The next few days' entries show that Friedbert and his letter were in the forefront of her mind, and she thought a lot about going to the Rhineland again. 'I bought a frame and put Friedbert's photograph on my desk so that I can see it when I'm working.'

> *Tues 24th April:* Went to the flicks with Pedley after supper – 2 Silly Symphonies, a Laurel and Hardy, and *Whither Germany?* which affected me greatly.

> *Wed 25th April:* After tea I felt terribly depressed about Schools – but the mood gave way later to one of exuberance. I am just going to write to Friedbert.

On Friday 27 April, after another evening at Henry Harvey and Robert Liddell's flat at 86b Banbury Road, where 'Henry was rather rude' to her, Barbara got back to her college. 'I looked at my photo of Friedbert and said aloud "Oh my darling – it's you I love." I wonder.'

> *Sat 28th April:* When I went to 86 this evening Henry and Jock quarrelled rather a lot and I left in a furious temper with Henry. Also, I lost my swastika and burst into tears in the Banbury Road because of it.

In spite of this loss, she records on Monday 30 April, 'April has been a happy month and I am sorry to see it go.'

> *Wed 2nd May:* At Bodley again. Henry came and spoke to me - they can't find my swastika - Jockie said so too. I am fed up…very depressed about work and a disquieting feeling that I may be in love with Gabriel still. I wish Friedbert would write, that would cheer me.

> *Thurs 3rd May:* If Friedbert does not write soon I shall find myself as deeply in love with Henry as ever I was before.

It seems as though she is here secretly playing off the two men against each other. When Henry is nice to her, Friedbert fades into the background, but when, inevitably it seems, he turns nasty and is rude to her, she pines for the polite and considerate Friedbert. And whenever Henry is away, she only thinks of his good side:

> *Sat 12th May:* I went to London again for the NUS reunion party…quite a lot of the actual people who'd been on the tour were there together with some Belgians and Germans who had been invited for the evening…there were some nice snaps about. I got hold of a lovely enlargement of me and Hanns on board the Rhine steamer – artistically grouped with 8 bottles in the foreground – glasses raised and all smiling. 'Promoting International Goodwill' I called it.

> *Tues 15th May:* I tried all over Oxford to get a swastika and was unsuccessful – except for a gold one which was too expensive. Oh dear – darling Friedbert, why don't you write? I want so terribly to go to Germany again and I'm 12/10d overdrawn at the Bank.

> I die for a letter or something from F. Gluck.

The following week: 'Not seeing Henry isn't really very good for me. How sentimental I get about him these days, every evening without fail. Now if only God would arrange that Friedbert would write to me things mightn't be so bad. But as it is I can only conclude that F. meant not a word he said or wrote (possible) or that I've offended him (vaguely possible) or perhaps I didn't translate his letter rightly, or – lots of things. Anyway I have very little faith in mankind now although

Hope *does* spring eternal in the human breast, especially in Sandra's!'
[Sandra was a name Barbara had invented for herself.]

> *Sat 26th May:* No work all day – a passionate desire to go to Germany.
>
> *Mon 28th May:* Had a very affectionate letter from Hanns Woischnik written in good English with many darlings in it. Apparently F. has told him that I am 'going there' in June – if so I wish F. would write! I did not realize that Hanns was at all fond of me. He says he will never forget me, but seems to think I am irretrievably Friedbert's! I suppose the truth is that I belong to a cruel, sweet Englishman called Henry Stanley Harvey, but at the age of not quite 21, it is not possible to be certain. Henry does not write, nor do I see him. The Germans, at least, appreciate me if the English don't…I do want to go back to Germany.

On Friday 1 June she had supper again with Jock and Henry. 'It was lovely – Henry said I looked blonde and Aryan, like something on the cover of *Die Woche*!' [a German weekly magazine.]

Under this entry is written 'Goodbye Twenty', and the next page is taken up with the words HERE BEGIN YEARS OF DISCRETION.

> *Sat 2nd June:* My 21st Birthday
>
> *Thurs 7th June:* Schools. I got my second.
>
> *Tues 19th June:* The first day on the Dole…I want to go to Germany on the last day of term. I had a nice letter from Friedbert.
>
> *Sat 30th June:* In the evening I found a letter from Friedbert awaiting me. [It appears that he was trying to find some sort of job for her in Germany – tutoring in a family, one imagines.] Now arrangements are to be made for me to go in September (D.V.) Links [Barbara and Hilary's nickname for their mother] isn't at all keen that I should go to a family purely on his recommendation, which is understandable, and I got very worried about what I should do about it…

Barbara was always a keen listener to the radio, and on 2 July she wrote,

'Some interesting talks on the wireless – about events in Germany – from Berlin by an Irishman...' That would surely have been William Joyce, derisively known in Britain as Lord Haw-Haw, who broadcast Nazi propaganda to Britain before and throughout the war. As he also held US citizenship it was possible for him to be tried for treason, for which he was hanged in 1946.

> *Sat 7th July:* ...negotiations about Germany still going on, but nothing definite is emerging from it yet. I still desire passionately to go there, and am still trying to acquire more vocabulary. I am reading some Goethe in the Oxford Book of German Verse. Tonight I cut out Nazi Germany cuttings ...at present my thoughts are most on Germany.
>
> *Wed 10th July:* Today I thought sadly of Friedbert. I'm not going to Cologne now, but perhaps to Hamburg with the NUS. Perhaps it would be dangerous to see him again. I thought of him at the very first lunch in Cologne making a speech in his black uniform. Life is sad but sometimes very romantic.

There are no diary entries between 26 July and 1 September. However it later appears that she did go to Hamburg, presumably with the student group, on 17 August. And it may have been after this that she and Hilary went on to Budapest.

At the end of July or early August she must have written to Rupert Gleadow, because in a letter from him dated 3 August he replied 'Really I feel quite jealous of you going to Budapest becos [sic] I've been wanting to go there for some time, finding the Hungarians an amusing race, and it is now 10 years since I spent a mere 2 days there... One can not under any circumstances love a *real* Nazi. Yours I'm sure must be only a pretence. The real ones (and I've been arrested by them!) are all sadists and keep their women brutally in order. But lots of Germans are very nice for all that.'

It wasn't until 1 September that Barbara wrote in her diary:

> Germany was delightful and more than usually interesting as we arrived in Hamburg on the same day as the Führer and were able to see him. I thought he looked smooth and clean and was

very impressed. The elections [a referendum to approve Hitler's becoming supreme head of state] were to be held on the Sunday, August 19th. There was plenty of publicity urging voters to say '*Ja*' for Hitler.

She does not mention Friedbert, who was presumably still in Cologne, on that visit.

On 1 September Barbara also wrote, 'Some time in July I began writing a story about Hilary and myself as spinsters of fiftyish. Henry, Jock and all of us appeared in it.' This, of course, was the first version of *Some Tame Gazelle*. What is less well known is that Friedbert also appeared briefly in it. She envisaged a situation in which the Nazis had been defeated and the exiles were living in poverty in Africa; Barbara (later Belinda) and her friends were knitting vests and things to send to them:

> Of course, it had been rather extravagant of her to use such an expensive wool to knit a charity garment, but she excused herself by remarking that after all the Nazis were rather 'special people.' Friedbert [later Helmut] had been a Nazi. She was wondering whether to wear her little Swastika brooch or not. Dear Friedbert had been so pleased at this sign of her presumable sympathy with the National Socialist Party.... Liebfraumilch always reminded Barbara of the Rhineland which she had visited in the spring when she was 20. The Nazis were young and arrogant then and she had hardly known which she liked best, Hanns [later Kurt] or Friedbert.... Barbara had always thought that Friedbert would make a good Führer, and much handsomer than Hitler.

Of course, none of this appeared in the published version of *Some Tame Gazelle*.

Henry had gone to Finland on 19 September and hadn't written to her:

> *Thurs 4th October:* I still love him very deeply as far as one is able to judge, with no men to compare him with and absence making the heart grow fonder...

On 20 October, she had another letter from Rupert Gleadow:

> It's good that you have been to Germany and can talk about it.

Oh, but *please* don't admire those *filthy* Nazis in their beautiful uniforms: you won't get a chance much longer, becos [sic] 1936 will just about see the end of Hitler. I think from your style you've had another love affair in the last few months? I suppose you are as chaste as ever?

On Good Friday, 19th April 1935, Barbara went to Cologne again with the NUS. 'I travelled to Dover with Michie and her friend Barbara Sparkes, who is very nice and can speak German…there were more women this year than last, but I didn't concern myself much over that…Arrived Brussels 6.16 – dinner and tour of town.' They left at 10 pm and arrived in Cologne about 6 am on the Saturday. 'I was very tired, but sufficiently awake to notice who of last year's German students were there to meet us. I noticed Müller and then, to my pleasure, Hanns. It was so nice to see his familiar face again that I felt comforted although there was no sign of Friedbert. We stayed at the *Kameradschafthaus.*' Very little more, except that on the next page, undated, Barbara wrote 'Friedbert was angelic to me. Such kindness as his one can never forget.'

> *May:* After Germany I was in love with Friedbert in a way. I put it so because I realized even at the time that most of it was probably glamour – his being a foreigner – the little Americanisms in his speech like 'terribly' and the way he said 'Barbara' – it being in a foreign country with the *Höhenzollern Brücke* by moonlight and *zwei* Manhattans at the Excelsior, and his Nivea cream that I rubbed on my arm to remember the smell of him – our evening of love in *Volkspartenstrasse zwei und fünfzig* – for all these things I loved him and yet I hardly knew him as a person and didn't at all agree with his National Socialism, although I tried to read Feuchtwänger's book *The Oppermans*… My interest in the language was reawakened with the result that I really learnt a good deal more.

But Henry's influence is always stronger. 'Now that I've seen Henry again I suppose it will be Swedish, which he seems to speak and read fluently and gets quite annoyed when I can't do the same.'

Sat 16th Nov: No letters today or indeed any other day it

seems. Henry, Jockie, Barnicot, Friedbert, Sharp [another St Hilda's student], London *Mercury* [a magazine to which Barbara had offered some short stories] – all silent.

There is no record of a visit to Germany in 1936, but in a letter to Henry reproaching him for not writing, she mentions that, 'Even Friedbert has spared a moment from the organization of the Olympic Games to send me a beautiful postcard.' If Friedbert was involved in the Games, and we heard earlier that he was good at sport, he may not have been free to meet Barbara that summer. She was obviously still thinking a lot about him though, because she mentions 'vivid and lovely dreams of Friedbert'. However, Henry came to the fore once again when in June and July Barbara was working as his secretary, for '30/- a week and a few caresses'.

There are no diary entries for the time that that Barbara was in Germany in 1937. It appears from letters that they (Barbara and Hilary?) went to the Black Forest. 'Tonight,' she writes to Jock, 'I have been drinking beer to get into practice for the large quantities we shall consume there…We are going…on 1st August….I shall be home again about 20th Aug.' This seems too long for a NUS tour, but we have no details of this trip. It has to be assumed that they met up with Friedbert.

On Sunday 12 December 1937 Henry Harvey married Elsie Godenhjelm in the English Church in Helsinki, Finland. Barbara inscribed in her journal, '*So endete eine grosse Liebe.*'

Early in the New Year of 1938, Barbara and Friedbert were in correspondence again. Apparently they were planning for her to visit him in Dresden where he was now stationed, and to stay almost a month. She wrote to Elsie Harvey on Easter Sunday, speaking of herself in the third person as she often did. 'She is making plans for visiting a foreign country, and dreaming at night of somebody she loves very much. But it is not anybody you know, so she will not tell you any boring details.'

This visit is recorded in pencil in a tiny diary, one page per day. Unlike her 1934 diary, she writes very little of her private feelings, confining herself almost entirely to fact.

On Tuesday 3 May she left for Germany, travelling via Aachen, Cologne and Leipzig, arriving about 10 the next morning in Dresden, where Friedbert met her, and took her to the room he had found for her, which she seemed to like very much. They had lunch together but because Friedbert had a sore throat and was feverish, she had dinner alone in her room and went to bed early. Friedbert was in bed all the next day, so she didn't see him, but he phoned her.

On the Friday she visited some museums. Friedbert, still not quite re-covered, met her at 5.30 at the Eden Hotel, where they read the English papers and had coffee, and later had supper in her room.

The next day, Saturday, Friedbert had to go away somewhere, so Bar-bara saw very little of him for the first four days of her holiday, but he returned in time for lunch on Sunday, after which 'We went to Pillnitz by train, walked about there and had coffee in a very nice café overlook-ing Dresden. After supper we went to Der Maulkart at the Regina Palast and afterwards had some beer at Zum Schwarzwälder.' You will note that no meal or drink ever goes unrecorded on this visit!

Friedbert did not take any leave during her visit, and indeed was away on duty on a number of occasions, when Barbara had to entertain her-self. However, there was a general pattern to their days. Barbara went sight-seeing in the mornings, Friedbert usually joining her for lunch in her room, which was presumably supplied by her landlady. He then went back to work, and met her later, sometimes even after dinner time, and then they would go out to bars and cafes, often until quite late:

Mon 9th May: F. came to lunch. Had tea at Rumpelmayers and supper at home with F. We then went to the Olympic Games film [no doubt the famous film made by Leni Riefenstahl] at the Prinzess Theatre. Very good. Then some beer at Zum Schwarzwälder.

Tues 10th May: Lazy morning. F. came to lunch and I walked with him to the tram stop...[he] came very late to supper and we went out to meet friends of his, Walter Naumann and a girl called Inge. We drank a lot – Rhine wine and cocktails...then had something to eat. Then to the Regina Palast where we had champagne and danced till nearly 3. Not much sleep that night.

Wed 11th May: Felt very tired…F. came to lunch. I slept in the afternoon then to the Eden where I met Friedbert and Walter. Then we went in Walter's car to a spot outside Dresden and walked a bit and then came back to my room for supper.

Thurs 12th May: F. didn't come to lunch but afterwards he took me in a car into the town and we had tea at a café…We had supper together and then stayed in my room until he left at about 11.30.

It is all beginning to sound rather dull and repetitive. But a visit to Prague was being planned:

Fri 13th May: F. came very late from Leipzig. We went out to the Alt Bayern Beergarten and made plans about going to Prague next day.

Barbara's diary account of this weekend visit is somewhat laconic:

Sat 14th May: Packed my small bag. I went to the station and got the tickets. Friedbert came just in time, 12.36. Train full and very hot. We had lunch, then sat in the dining car for coffee. Passed through the lovely Sächsische Scharz to the frontier at Bodenbach. Then into Czechoslovakia…we got to Prague about 4. Went to the Hotel Bevanek. Doppel Zimmer. Had a bath. Walked about. Ate at restaurant Procheski, wandered in Wenceslas Square…then bed quite early.

Sun 15th May: Had breakfast 8.30 then sightseeing tour of the town which lasted until after 1. Saw very much. Very hot. Lunch at Deutsche Haus. Packed and left hotel. Had coffee in the town, then caught the 5 o/c train – carriage to ourselves. F. slept. I had ham and eggs in the dining car…got to Dresden after 8.

But in a letter to Jock on 23 May she was more expansive:

Did I tell you that we went to Prague the weekend before last?…It was as hot as August and we sat in the restaurant car mopping our faces and making rather waspish remarks to each

food at the Baren Schauke. Also looked at the Elbe. Came home, had a talk, and parted friends.

– which might suggest that there was a falling out earlier.

During her last weekend Friedbert was away all day on Saturday and most of Sunday. Barbara met his train at 9 pm. On Monday 30 May, the day before she left, her entry is enigmatic. 'F. came to supper. Went to his room while he typed a letter. Then to the Weindorf in Prägerstr. Very nice. Then mock turtle soup at the station. I chased my hat down Uhlenstr. at 4am.'

That was the last time she saw him. He did not come to the station to see her off the next day, probably because he couldn't leave the office. Barbara wrote in her diary, 'June 1st – Henry's 27th birthday. Shopped in the morning, and in the afternoon a last visit to the Eden…Went home and packed, had my last meal in my dear room. Left at 8.34. Many soldiers on the train, all very nice to me. Slept quite a lot.' Not a mention of Friedbert. She was still on her journey home on her 25th birthday.

In August she went to Katowice in Poland to teach English to Ula Alberg, but because of the worsening political situation Dr Alberg sent her home in October. Evidently she did not meet with Friedbert on either journey.

Throughout 1939 Barbara's diary tells of the seriousness of the international situation, until they heard on 1 September that Hitler had taken Danzig and invaded Poland:

> Bombed many towns including Katowice…[Fortunately the Jewish Albergs got out in time and went to England.] Spent day making blackout curtains…Everyone cheerful. Constant news bulletins. Our Ambassador at 9.40 pm gave a note to Germany saying that unless hostilities ceased and troops withdrawn we should fulfill our obligations.
>
> *Sun 3rd Sep:* We gave Hitler until 11am to withdraw from Poland and at 11.15 Mr. Chamberlain spoke to the nation and told us that we were now at war with Germany.

On 12 Jan 1940, Barbara wrote to Jock, 'I have no recent news of Friedbert for you as I have not written to him since September – nor he to me…One does not expect letters from enemy aliens…'

On Wednesday 10 April she remembers that it is Friedbert's 29th birthday.

Sunday 26 May was a day of national prayer. 'Church packed morning and evening. 2 fine sermons. I thought, "Friedbert, against this, you haven't a chance".'

Just after the Germans had declared war on Yugoslavia and Greece in April 1941, it was Friedbert's birthday again and Barbara wrote in her diary 'I put a vase of spring flowers by the portrait of one who may be in the Balkans and whom I shall always love.' However, Hazel Holt thinks that this refers to Julian Amery.

By November, Barbara had applied for work in to the Censorship Department. 'Started brushing up my German – reading poor F.'s letters.' Throughout the month she was assiduously studying German, 'Reading Goethe's letters,' and 'Struggling over Rilke – perhaps Friedbert was right about my not being able to understand him.' And on Tuesday 18 November: 'After tea, translating a letter from Friedbert, one of the last I had and painful to me. One feels one ought to be ashamed of ever having been fond of a German. Where are you now?'

Hazel Holt tells us in *A Lot To Ask* that in December Hilary heard from Nora Wahn, who had written several books on Nazi Germany, and was working at the BBC, that Friedbert had 'gone anti-Nazi,' but as Hazel says 'It is hard to imagine how an SS officer could have done this and survived.'

Even as late as 1943, Barbara still sometimes thought of Friedbert. In a letter to Henry from Bristol she says, 'I was tidying a drawer this evening and came across a photo of poor Anton Feudrich! [A mutual friend who used to live in England.] I wonder where he is now – also my dear Friedbert…' and on Sunday 24 October in London, 'went to a big Lyons where I got a seat at a table with two young men – (one very dark and good looking, who reminded me of poor Friedbert).'

There are no further references to him in the diaries until after the war. As the appalling events in Germany were gradually revealed, the feeling of shame at having known and loved a Nazi must have intensified, and Barbara would not have wanted anyone to know about this episode in her life. Friedbert evidently survived, for on 31 July 1946, over a year after the end of the war in Europe, and again on 24 September, her diary records letters from him, but their contents are destined to remain unknown. Even Hilary was not aware of them. It is unlikely that Barbara responded. The romantic dream was finally shattered by stark reality, and another great love ended.

An earlier version of this paper was presented at the 2006 North American Conference in Cambridge, Massachusetts.

5

Some Tame Gazelle:
Some Views and Reviews

1949 – 1950

Sometime in July I began to write a story about
Hilary and me as spinsters of fiftyish.
Henry and Jock and all of us appeared in it. I sent it
to them and they liked it very much.
So I am going on with it and some day it may
become a book.

5

Some Tame Gazelle: *Some Views and Reviews*

When I started reading Barbara's papers in the Bodleian library back in 2001 I was impressed by the large number of fan letters she received from complete strangers, saying how much they enjoyed her books, and usually asking when she was to publish the next. Most of these, of course, came during Barbara's 'wilderness' years, when her fans simply could not understand why Barbara had stopped writing. After *Quartet in Autumn* came out one admirer even wrote, 'I am SO glad that you are not dead. I was SO dreadfully sorry when you suddenly stopped writing, and could see no reason other than demise.'

As I was reading these letters, I thought it might be interesting to compile some of the contemporary opinions of *Some Tame Gazelle* expressed by friends, fans and reviewers. Since this was a first novel, there were not many of the 'fan' type letters, but her friends were fulsome in their praise, and there was a remarkable consensus among her admirers.

Barbara Pym's earliest attempts to have *Some Tame Gazelle* published were unsuccessful, but in August 1936 Jonathan Cape did express some interest if she were prepared to make certain changes. Barbara did so, but was gravely disappointed when Jonathan Cape changed his mind and rejected it with what I thought a rather limp excuse: 'I fear…we should be unable to give it all the care and attention which I feel are necessary if it is to be successfully launched.'

Barbara put the novel aside and turned her mind to other projects. With the advent of war, all thoughts of pursuing her writing career had to be put aside, and it was not until 1949 that she sent an amended manuscript to Jonathan Cape. This time he readily accepted the novel.

Barbara's friends were, of course, delighted when *Some Tame Gazelle* was published in May 1950, and many wrote to say so. Some simply offered congratulations and expressed their pleasure at her success. Others gave their opinions on plot and characters. One of the earliest letters I found was from an old friend, Frances Atkin, who went rather over the top in her boundless enthusiasm:

> Dearest Barbara
>
> For 3 days I've been trying to think of the most 'suitable' way to begin my fan letter to you, but the moment I start thinking about *Some Tame Gazelle* I get a terrific rush of superlatives to the brain and I start getting incoherent.
>
> It is a joy – something warm, comforting and rewarding. I adored every word of it and can't wait to get it back from my mother to read it again. I indulge in nice reminiscent chuckles from time to time...
>
> It is not only extremely funny but, at times, very touching and profound. I will never be able to tell you of the pure joy and delight which reading it gave me, but as so few enjoyments in life are quite unclouded and unspoilt, will you take it on trust that the first reading of *Some Tame Gazelle* was one of those rare and treasured experiences? Future readings, and there will be many, though they might not have the delicious tang of the first enchantments, will have the cosiness of respectful intimacy.

Elizabeth Barnicot, whose husband John was the model for Nicholas Parnell, wrote:

> We've both read your book already and we both love it. Of course I'm putting it on my list at Boots, and getting all my friends to do the same, so as to create a demand, but everyone is asking to borrow it...
>
> I enjoyed it all and could hardly put it down. In fact, It does what novels rarely do – goes from strength to strength.

Gordon Glover, with whom Barbara had been in love in the early forties and who had now married for the second time, wrote on May Day:

> As we are going for the day to London we will make a point of obtaining *Some Tame Gazelle* – or is it 'lame' gazelle? – and will read it with assured satisfaction.

About a week later he confirmed:

> Your *Tame Gazelle*, Barbara. dear, arrived here on Saturday morning…I think It is quite, quite delightful – Hoccleve and Mbawawa are beautiful creations and I thought the whole thing flowed along as easily and prettily and wittily and non-distressingly as one could wish. Only character in whom I could not altogether believe was Bianco, and perhaps I felt that the village itself was a little bit vague – couldn't quite picture it as to size, venue and so on. But that is perhaps an unfair criticism of an altogether delightful conversation piece.

Another male friend, who had presumably discussed the book earlier with Barbara, wrote irreverently:

> I liked your Gazelle and finished it by agreeing with you that Belinda was really rather a silly little thing who should have had her bottom smacked (or alternatively had a night with the milkman) at an early age. But it was all great fun and I enjoyed it. I was a bit shattered by *The Observer* who said you were a bit like Trollope – whom I cannot abide. I was continually surprised by its unsophistication.

This next letter is from a lady who does not express herself very well, but I think we can understand and agree with what she is trying to say:

> I expect you are tired of letters about your Tame Gazelle but perhaps one doesn't tire easily of hearing that one's book has been liked. I do like it very much, its modest attitude and kindness are so pleasant and unusual and the smiles without feeling malicious, which is a rare pleasure. The Archdeacon is unique – you have got his detachment and the curious immunity from blame which he bears, so that his friends are driven to blaming themselves for condemning him and almost feel they ought to do 'outrageous' things if he asks them to…

It wasn't until September that Barbara's first true love, Henry Harvey, wrote. He was now married for the second time, and he quotes from a rather curious letter that Susi, his German wife, had written to him about *Some Tame Gazelle*. Susi clearly has an ambivalent attitude towards Barbara, resenting Henry's continuing interest in her, but admiring the novel in spite of herself:

> I think it is due to Barbara's book that I feel so happy. It is a good book in the human sense of the word…I started it yesterday…and at first was rather annoyed with a kind of amateurish clumsiness in style and the occasional thinness, almost shabbiness. I suppose I was a little annoyed about the extraordinary claim she has on you too. But soon she caught me; the book gets fuller and richer towards the middle, the flow smoother. It certainly is good in another than the human sense too. She talks about food and clothes and a few odd people, quotes bits of poetry (only too well known to me!), describes day after day instant after instant, without anything surprising happening, without sensational gossip, without even painting the characters very clearly or giving interesting details of their psyches and subconscious movements – and still she fascinates from the beginning to the end. What a good heart she must have! I don't ever want to meet her. She moved me to tears when I finished it this morning.

C. K. Meek, an anthropologist from Nigeria who was a frequent visitor to the International African Institute, wrote,

> Dear Barbara,
>
> I just wish to say how much I have enjoyed reading *Some Tame Gazelle*. It is most pleasantly written and I enjoyed the fun you poke at anthropology, including two passages which were clearly written under the boredom of having to wade through my "Sudanese Kingdom[1]."…A friend of mine to whom I gave a copy says, 'I have read *Some Tame Gazelle* and liked it very much. I have lived in a village all my life and the book gives a very true picture of the things that go on in a small place.'

The last letter I have selected, though not written until 1977, is quite moving, the more so, perhaps, because the writer was a man:

> Dear Miss Pym,
>
> The *Times Literary Supplement* article put me on to your books. I've enjoyed reading all of them, but for some reason I like best *Some Tame Gazelle* which I happened to read last. I was about

two thirds of the way through when my father died of cancer. This was my first experience of death. We spent his last 26 hours at his bedside. My first return to anything which wasn't mourning or turmoil was the last third of *Some Tame Gazelle* and I don't think I could have had a better balm for the spirit. To me in that situation each sentence seemed to drop its quiet grace, especially 'but the place where they stood was reassuringly filled with dried Cape gooseberries and honesty.' Thank you for the books and for the special help of *Some Tame Gazelle*.

Public acclaim came in the form of reviews from a wide range of newspapers and magazines, local and national, even international. Reggie Smith wrote,

Dear Miss Pym

I'm sorry to say that CIRCUS for which I hoped to review your book has collapsed, or more accurately, has been overturned.

Thereby hangs an interesting tale, no doubt, but we are told no more! He goes on:

I did enjoy the book, and wish I could review it; and if my wife Olivia Manning hasn't done it for the *Palestine Post* I will.

Pamela Hansford Johnson wrote a review for the *Daily Telegraph*, but it is not in the archive. L. A. G. Strong, a well-known author and reviewer at that time, did one for the *Spectator*, and Antonia White one for the *New Statesman and Nation*, and no doubt there were others.

Some shorter reviews and notices are recorded, but mainly without attribution, like this one:

If this novel comes scratching at your front door, let the playful little thing come in. Do not be discouraged by the news that it deals with mild flirtations in the vicarage and, in particular, Belinda's 30 years of faithful love for an archdeacon and Harriet's almost (but not quite) maternal feelings for the new curate.

For this novel is in a sturdy English tradition of comedy. Its wit is so gentle that the reader scarcely notices the claws. How

hard, for instance, to realise that handsome Archdeacon Hoccleve with his literary sermons is being coolly but decisively
exhibited as a figure of fun.

Strongly recommended to all who liked Angela Thirkell in her
palmy days.

However, another reviewer disagreed:

Some Tame Gazelle is as restrained as its title suggests, and describes the relations of an archdeacon in a small country town
with his wife and female parishioners. Apart from an excellent
parody of a 'literary' sermon, the book flows cheerfully on with
little wit and much incident, and many readers will compare it
unfavourably with the earlier novels of Mrs Thirkell.

That was the only one I found in that disparaging vein. All the others
liked the novel, and seemed to appreciate the same virtues in it.

This one is entitled 'Fun and Scholarship':

Some Tame Gazelle is really very funny indeed. I may have been
in a singularly happy mood when I read it, but I found it quite
uproariously funny at the time. It is the story of two charming
maiden ladies; one of them cherishes a comfortable, harmless
romantic passion for the absurd Archdeacon Hoccleve, and the
other expends her tenderness upon curates.

There is a touch of Trollope here, of Mrs Gaskell, Jane Austen
and Mrs Thirkell, but Miss Pym's sharp fresh fun is all her own,
and her mild vein of ribaldry turns to pure joy the account
of the lecture given in the village hall by the Bishop from
Mbawawa.

There is also an amiable air of scholarship about this novel
which I find most pleasing...[It] made me very happy for an
entire afternoon.

An interesting observation on the novel's potential readership is made
by this reviewer:

This excellent first novel on a theme of English village life is in
the direct tradition of Jane Austen, Trollope and E. M. Dela-
field.

To those who appreciate such a background, its quiet and good-humoured ironies will bring great delight, especially the rich comedy of the vicarage garden party, the visit of Miss Prior (the 'little sewing woman') and, above all, the lantern lecture, given by the Bishop of Mbawawa.

To those, on the other hand, who have no knowledge of this social background, it will probably seem as 'foreign' as a novel by Dostoevsky and as 'peculiar' as a short story by Chekhov.

Most of the reviewers made comparisons between Barbara's work and that of other authors. Philip Day thought her 'lively, witty, sympathetic study of village, and particularly clerical, life' was 'Cranfordish,' being 'astringently attractive, often really funny.'

Another reviewer felt that 'She has applied Jane Austen's method to contemporary life.'

Again:

Archdeacons, village spinsters, garden-parties, gossips and pale curates are the endearing substance of *Some Tame Gazelle*, in which Miss Barbara Pym has compounded something of Trollope, something of Jane Austen, something of *Cranford*, and (where the willowy young clergy are concerned) more than a little of the Punch of the 1890s...

I should like to end with Antonia White's review in the *New Statesman and Nation* for 1 July 1950. Hazel Holt quoted a passage from it in *A Lot to Ask*, but I think it is worth citing in full, not only for the quality of its writing, but for her perceptive appreciation of Barbara's novel.

The ingredients of *Some Tame Gazelle* might suggest that the novel itself was tame. Miss Barbara Pym presents us with one of those English villages where the community is bound together by a passionate interest in the details of each member's daily life. The trimming of a hat, the question of who shall 'do' the pulpit for the Harvest Festival, even the amount of luggage the vicar's wife will take on her holiday, furnish speculative conversation for weeks. For characters she offers us two spinster sisters – one rather dashing, one faded and shy – a curate, an archdeacon and a handful of middle-aged characters, lay and clerical, who knew each other in youth and still share jokes and quotations from their Oxford days. The result, however, is far from tame. Not because anything sensational happens, but because Miss Pym, working in *petit point*, makes each stitch with perfect precision. She keeps her designs so perfectly to scale, and places one mild tint in such happy juxtaposition to another, that this reader, at any rate, derived considerable pleasure from it.

Over and over again, I thought Miss Pym, skating over such thin and conventional ice, might tumble through into a pool of Miniverism, but she skims over it dry-shod. Her portraits of the three clergymen, Curate, Archdeacon, and Colonial Bishop, are gentle but relentless, as a conscientious snapshot can be more devastating than the cruellest caricature. She is scrupulously fair to her characters; she allows the likable to be irritating and the unlikable to have charm. If she mocks the preposterous selfishness of handsome Archdeacon Hoccleve, she also mocks sensitive, ineffectual Belinda Bede who cannot break the habit of being in love with him.

Miss Pym will almost certainly – and not without reason – be compared to Jane Austen, and very possibly to Trollope. My own impression is that she is a modest and original writer who owes nothing to anyone. If my first sip of *Some Tame Gazelle* suggested that this was merely a pale mixed cup such as might be served at the vicarage garden party, my second convinced me that it was an authentic wine. Not everyone's wine, perhaps, not one that 'travels well' in the reviewing, but with a bouquet of its own and more body than you might suspect from its lightness.

An earlier version of this paper was presented at the 2001 Annual General Meeting in Oxford.

6

Mildred's World:
The Making of Excellent Women

1949 – 1952

I suppose an unmarried woman just over thirty,
who lives alone and has no apparent ties,
must expect to find herself involved or interested in
other people's business, and if she is also
a clergyman's daughter then one might really say
that there is no hope for her.

Mildred's World:
The making of Excellent Women

Barbara did not express any pleasure or excitement in her notebooks at the publication of *Some Tame Gazelle*, which was surely a pivotal moment in her literary life. Now that I think about it, I don't remember her showing in her diaries or notebooks much pleasure on publication of any of her novels, although her disappointment when they were rejected is sometimes recorded. Perhaps she confined her feelings to correspondence or conversations with her friends and admirers.

However, as we see from her notebook for 1948-9, she began thinking about her next novel around the same time as *Some Tame Gazelle* was accepted by Cape, in March 1949.

Jottings from the notebook include the following entries, most of which found their way into the finished novels:

Seen from the top of a bus – a woman and a clergyman sitting on hard chairs in Green Park, and talking with animation. [Sitting on] Deck chairs even worse.

When Dora came to stay she had tea rather than coffee after meals. The hairnet on the mantelpiece, the bulging canvas bag, the penetrating glance.

Excellent women enjoying discomfort – one bar of a small electric fire, huddled in coats. [Though a second bar of the electric fire could be turned on in an emergency, as when Winifred, inadequately dressed, arrives one night at Mildred's in the rain, soaking wet.]

The electricity man comes – has to check among the swinging wet stockings and knickers but the expression of his serious rather worried blue eyes does not change. [In the end it was Rocky, not an electrician, who edged his way, without comment, beneath Dora's dreary undies, though on another occasion, when the clothes were dry, he did make jokes about them.]

As a vicar's daughter it was too late for me to change.

Men should be given the opportunity for self sacrifice as they are in their natures so much less noble than women. (I wonder if Mrs Grey, the widow, tends to make rather clever remarks like this, and so antagonise Mildred?)

Wife of distinguished anthropologist quietly sleeping through his lecture.

In the 1950 notebook, Barbara develops some of these themes, and introduces new characters:

I go out shopping with Dora and we see Allegra and Fr. Malory sitting on deckchairs in the park. [An image that Barbara particularly seems to enjoy.]

Then Allegra asks me to lunch with her – I wonder why? She eats little and makes me feel inferior…what is to be done with Winifred – can she live with me?

Then I go and see R[ocky] and tell him about it – he sympathises and I feel angry and humiliated…he tries to comfort me.

At the end when the Napiers leave, Miss Edgar and Miss Boniface take their flat. Miss E calls her Bony – want to have their own toilet paper and a rota for cleaning the bath.

Dora and I go down to the old school to the dedication of some hideous stained glass window in memory of a late headmistress…so and so has done well. She looks smart but she hasn't married – isn't that really the point. Somebody else had, when all hope may have been past, but what is he? Some little clergyman.

The sticky tea with Julian and Rocky. I am nervous – it flows in an 'amber stream,' much too weak…both Rocky and Julian appear in a bad light.

On holiday Dora and I go to see Buckfast Abbey. Monk who shows us round is condescending about Our Lady. Group of indignant Anglo-catholic ladies begin whispering together.

I see two priests in the No. 9 queue failing to get on the bus. Serve them right because of the Pope's new dogma! [Presumably the Assumption of Mary, proclaimed by Pope Pius XII on 1 November 1950.]

'A man has a joking relationship with his in-laws which goes so far that he may sleep with a sister-in-law who is visiting the house.'

'I don't think that's much of a joke,' said R, 'though it might be fun. It will depend on the sister-in-law.'

Helena and Everard said nothing. They did not like jokes about anthropology.

Barbara took these notes and made a first draft of her novel. This is contained in an exercise book, which was later bound. It is headed 'A full life'.

In brief it is the story of a woman – a pleasant humorous spinster in the middle thirties – who gets continually embroiled in other people's affairs. The set-up is as follows – she lives in a flat in a house (somewhere like Pimlico) which has two or three flats – not self-contained. She first meets Mrs Mogden (Eleanor) when she is carrying down the rubbish. Mrs M., married to a naval officer who has been in Naples, moves in. They have a house in the country in a village adjoining the one where the spinster's father was a vicar. Think the flat rather awful but the best they can do – they have some 'nice things.' While her husband was in Naples Mrs M. was doing anthropological work (in Nigeria perhaps) with a fellow anthropologist. Mr M. has met a nice wren whom he wants to marry so he tries to divorce his wife citing the anthropologist. The spinster gets involved. After getting to know them first she's asked down to their cottage and is made to write letters about furniture. In addition, she's much concerned with church matters – the vicar (Fr Somebody) lives with his sister in a large vicarage. He wants to get married and the sister, feeling she is turned out, comes to the spinster.

The anthropologist in the meantime is offered some position – but questions are asked about his relationship with Mrs M.

In the end, I should think, you have Mrs M, the vicar's sister and the spinster all living together somewhat uncomfortably until a relative writes to the spinster and begs for her services as a companion.

Characters (my readers will feel that I ought to be in love with the vicar). [Note that Barbara identifies herself with Mildred.]

The Spinster [Mildred Lathbury]. Middle thirties, daughter of low church vicar and wife, now dead. Has always had leanings towards High which she is now able to indulge. Humorous and intelligent. Has had one love affair, perhaps in late twenties. Why is she in London? She worked there at some missionary place perhaps, or did part-time secretarial work. Has small income.

Mrs M. [Helena Napier]. Attractive – early thirties – outspoken. Obstinate. Smokes a lot and I don't.

Mr M. [Rockingham Napier]. Conventional.

The Anthropologist [Everard Bone]. Attracted to Mrs M., respectable, pious perhaps. Selfish. Likes his food – small plover.

The Vicar [Julian Malory]. Nice, good-looking. Apologises for church not being old. Not much sense of humour.

Sister [Winifred Malory]. Much older. Ready to take offence. Ragbaggy in clothes.

Names

Mrs Dakers – Rockingham and Clarissa.

Mildred Lathbury

Fr Julian Malory, Winifred Malory, his sister

Miss Bodicote, Miss Statham, Miss Enders [dressmaker].

My daily woman Mrs Moffatt, rather like our Mrs Morris

Rough outline of chapters written so far

Cap I. First meeting with Mrs M. moving in and carrying rubbish down. I learn something of her circumstances and reveal something of mine.

Cap II. Supper with Winifred and Julian Malory. Their intention of letting part of the vicarage as a flat.

Cap III. Mrs Napier talks about Rockingham and Everard and gives a hint of their matrimonial differences.

Cap IV. Rockingham comes back and I get on well with him. Everard comes back with her. He and I talk together – I dislike him.

Cap V. Winifred and Julian – preparation for jumble sale and distempering the flat – news of the widow who has taken it.

Cap VI. The beginning of Lent and my seeing Everard Bone at the lunch hour service. Sight of Mrs Gray laughing with Julian.

Cap VII. Jumble sale. Meeting Mrs Gray.

Cap VIII. Lunch with William Caldicote.

Cap IX. Lent service again.

Cap X. The paper at the learned society.

Other matters to be included

Deaconess Blatt – splendid on her bicycle

Dora Caldicote to stay

A visit to Rocky's cottage

Mrs Gray unpacking her things

Remember that Mrs Morris is going to work for the Napiers and may provide some sidelights

Why should I not try to make Everard Bone marry Mrs Gray? And in the end Julian gets her, and Everard proposes to me?

The rest of this draft is largely in note form, but some chapters are written in detail. It ends with what was to become Cap XXIV. All characters are now established, and names decided. The visit to Rocky's cottage, and any liaison between Everard Bone and Allegra Gray were dropped in the final version.

There is another partial draft in a bound octavo notebook. It is hand written on rectos only, corrections being made on versos. This draft is continuous, i.e. not divided into chapters, and ends with the jumble sale.

A large third bound volume contains the typescript of the complete novel with publisher's amendments. Apparently Barbara did not keep drafts of the later chapters.

In her diary under 14 January 1950 Barbara notes 'Two and a half pages typed new novel', and on 21 February 1951 she sent the completed typescript to Cape. It was published on 3 March 1952.

Excellent Women was extremely well received by the press, and some very distinguished reviewers.

J. W. Lambert, writing in *The Sunday Times*, 2 March 1952, was the first.

> Miss Barbara Pym consolidated her claim, staked with *Some Tame Gazelle*, as a dry-point chronicler of scenes from semi-clerical life. Living with genteel moderation in that part of London which, if not precisely Pimlico, is by no means Belgravia, Mildred Lathbury, the narrator of *Excellent Women*, spins out a life of mild good works; it revolves round an association for helping distressed gentlewomen ('I might so easily become one myself'), and the local Anglo-Catholic church, and is diverted for a while by the affairs of a handsome naval officer and his wife, a brusque anthropologist. A witty, charming and sad little story: the sadness is an aftertaste, the wit and charm ever-present pleasures.

Marghanita Laski, a distinguished novelist herself, wrote in *The Observer* on 9 March 1952:

> I don't think I've ever before recommended a novel as one that everybody will enjoy, and yet – even with a certain assurance – I'm prepared to vouch for *Excellent Women*, in which a clergyman's daughter tells of her life with the local vicar and the female anthropologist, with the old school friend and with the handsome ex-naval officer, so enticing and yet so insecure. Of nothing could one be more chary than introducing Jane Austen's name into a review, and yet very tentatively, very hesitantly, taking it back as soon as given – well, there it is.

John Betjeman, who later became Poet Laureate, wrote in *The Daily Telegraph* on 14 March 1952:

> Barbara Pym is a splendid humorous writer. She knows her

limits and stays within them. She writes about that world that is much bigger than people suppose, of professional men – clergymen, doctors' widows, the higher but not the top grades of the Civil Service, naval officers and their wives, gentlewomen who are not quite distressed.

There are those who might find *Excellent Women* tame, with its fussing over church bazaars, 'high' and 'low' churchmanship, a boiled egg for lunch and a cup of tea before going to bed, but for me it is a perfect book...Miss Pym's chief characters, and her lesser ones, are all carefully observed and wittily described. She is not sarcastic but always dry and caustic. Conscious charm by a professional ladies' man, quarrelsomeness from an old school friend, rows about where to put the lilies in the chancel at Easter, are subjects which suit her acid powers of description. *Excellent Women* is England, and, thank goodness, it is full of them.

Among other reviews were Frederick Laws in *News Chronicle*, 7 March 1952:

You will enjoy *Excellent Women*. It is a quietly mischievous story of a clergyman's daughter whose known sensibleness lands her with the troubles of more picturesque people: ' "Oh, dear, one was to be forever cast down," I thought, brooding over the piece of fish on my plate. If I had been flattered by Everard's invitation to lunch, I was now put in my place as the kind of person who would have an oven cloth hanging on a nail by the side of the cooker.'

The piercing wit of gentle women is to be savoured with trembling. We needn't bring Jane Austen into it, but Miss Pym *is* writing in a great tradition and knows it.

The *Manchester Guardian* thought that

Miss Pym is an excellent woman herself in so far as she is an excellent writer. Her kind tittle-tattling Mildred is a shrewd observer of men and women, and though this is a mannered book, its humour is not superficial and the people of the story are very much alive.

The *Times Literary Supplement* on 28 March 1952 was quite impressed:

> From the mildly eventful parish life of an English village, Miss Pym turns to an Anglo-Catholic church somewhere behind Victoria Station. The narrator is Mildred Lathbury, a young spinster of means who works for distressed gentlewomen. Her amused detachment is continually being broken down by the minor emotional storms of her friends and acquaintances, and Miss Pym is really very funny about the tenants of the flat below, a naval officer of devastating charm and his anthropologist wife, who nearly get divorced. Miss Pym wears her religion without much self-consciousness, and the book shows a definite advance on her first novel *Some Tame Gazelle*.

The *Church Times* of 16 May 1952 was also enthusiastic:

> Light fiction of any quality is hard to find nowadays. But Miss Barbara Pym's *Excellent Women* provides the exception…It would have been so easy to have gently ridiculed Mildred Lathbury, and to have left it at that. Miss Pym allows the reader to observe her *gaucheries*, but leaves no doubt about her essential goodness…Occasionally this book reveals flashes of insight into female character worthy of Jane Austen.

There were further appreciative reviews when *Excellent Women* was reissued in 1977. Anne Duchêne wrote in the *Times Literary Supplement* on 30 September 1977:

> Of all her books *Excellent Women* still seems the most felicitous. Its heroine, the magnificent Mildred, rises blithely to embrace her singleness, endowed with graceful primness, natural piety and an unconquerable scepticism…Mildred's men are all rather regrettable. William, having offered the annual luncheon and made the usual fuss about the wine, stands beside her in Soho sunshine afterwards while she buys a bunch of mimosa; Father Malory takes it for granted her heart will be broken if he marries someone else; Everard Bone, the anthropologist, sees her as a voluntary indexer…

Elizabeth Harvey [Henry's sister] in the *Birmingham Post* on 23 September 1977:

Excellent Women, published in 1952, and now reprinted, has a splendidly diverting and original character in the narrator Mildred, one of those unmarried women living alone, much engaged in parish affairs, and having the Pym heroine's superb gift of looking closely at herself and laughing.

She admits enjoying other people's lives more than her own, and is glad she is not a man, the kind 'who looked on a meal alone as a good opportunity to cook a small plover'. Burdens in a way are a pleasure to her and she does not mind being remembered as a woman who was always making cups of tea. The wit, the sharp commonsensical judgments are characteristic of this author's unique manner of writing.

A. L. Rowse called his 19 October 1977 review in *Punch* 'Austen Mini':

I am very ill-read in contemporary novels. I just wait for 10 or 15 years until the chaff has settled, and then take the advice of someone who knows much better than I do. In this case that of Philip Larkin, and of Lord David Cecil who says that Barbara Pym's *Excellent Women* and *A Glass of Blessings* are 'for me the finest examples of high comedy to have appeared in England during the past 75 years'. That is, in this century – can that possibly be true?

Following their recent reissue, I decided to give them a try, and discover that she is very much my cup of tea – I could go on reading her forever.

Shirley Hazzard wrote:

Excellent Women is so entirely delightful that its tremor of pain takes the reader unaware. The novel's narrator is a woman in her thirties, pious, comely and kind, whose willingness merely to assist at other people's lives is taken for granted by her friends, and very nearly by herself…the heroine's [very worth practically ensures that she will be overlooked] – a risk that Miss Pym herself has fearlessly run and triumphed over with the excellence of this book.

Among Barbara's correspondence are letters about *Excellent Women* from friends and fans. One of the earliest, written from Giza, Egypt, on 27

March 1952, was from her great friend and supporter Robert Liddell, to whom Barbara had sent a complimentary copy of *Excellent Women*.

> Dearest Barbara
>
> Thank you so much for *Excellent Women*. Our publisher also sent me a copy…he told me it gave him a great personal satisfaction…I sincerely congratulate you – the tone is beautifully and faultlessly managed – one feels Mildred genuinely expects so little for herself that it is almost sad…the Napiers, Everard, William, Dora are all a great success – and church too, but why so few clergy?
>
> You must be relieved to have got over the stumbling-block of a second book so successfully. Having thought you the finest comic writer of the age for about 18 years, I am delighted to find that opinion becoming general.
>
> I returned tired to Cairo yesterday…there was EW – just at the fitting moment. As I had four teaching hours, four until eight, I decided to let Abd El Fattah bring me eggs and toast and honey and Ovaltine in bed, and to read EW there. It was a JOY. And how I rejoice to find a character called Rockingham.

The criminologist and author F. Tennyson Jesse, who wrote *A Pin to See the Peepshow* about the Thomson and Bywaters *cause célèbre*, sent this letter to Jonathan Cape on 6 August:

> I am sorry not to have written before about *Excellent Women* by Barbara Pym…I have read this book before and admired it, but I have read it again very carefully a second time…Barbara Pym knows her stuff. She doesn't overdo, as so many people do, the poor pious hens who hang around the vicarage and try to help 'the dear vicar'…
>
> What I admire about BP's writing, and admired so much when I first read the book, is her quiet restraint…The weakness and strength of that strange conglomeration known as the Church of England shows very clearly in her book, and always without a touch of exaggeration.
>
> I hope this book had a great success…it certainly deserved to have one. If at any time you are seeing Miss Pym, do give her

my congratulations. It is easy enough to write about dull people and make them dull. It is even easy enough to write about exciting people and make them dull. But it is very brilliant indeed to write about what most people would think were dull people and make them all absorbingly interesting. That is what she has achieved...It is beautifully done.

Elizabeth, wife of John Barnicot, a Bodleian librarian friend of Barbara, Henry and Robert, wrote:

Dear Barbara

For weeks I have been meaning to – and promising John to – write to you and tell you how much we have enjoyed *Excellent Women*. And how pleased we are to see that the critics – and the Book Society – and the BBC – all share our view. I like it even better than *Some Tame Gazelle*. If you will not think me a heretic I will confide that I regard your works more highly than Jock's, for, whereas he arranges his bits and pieces to make a pretty picture, you seem able to shine a light on a pattern that is already there under life's surface.

Another friend said:

On our way to Paddington we stopped at the Times Bookshop to buy Miss Pym's new book and were told 'Sorry, sold out – it is in great demand'. So we hurried to Bumpus and were told the same!

I don't think I have mentioned how *very much* we enjoyed *Excellent Women*. I was so cast down when I'd finished it, can't you write a sequel? I laughed and laughed over the Ladies' Cloak-room and the lipstick buying.

WH Smiths had done you proud – the window was full of it.

David Cox wrote in September:

Many thanks for lending me *Excellent Women* which I enjoyed immensely. I found it both entertaining and disturbing. I'm sure every *man* who reads it will ask himself: Am I very dull? Am I very inconsiderate? Do I like to imagine women are in love with me when they obviously aren't?

I like the way it's written very much. The style seems to me consistently good, clear, interesting, easy to read, and at the same time portrays perfectly the character of the narrator...I like Miss Lathbury and her sense of humour appeals to me very much! ...

I shall certainly buy several copies at Christmas time and give them to people who I know will enjoy it very much also.

A stranger, Dorothy Jowitt, sent this from Winchester on 7 June 1952:

Dear Mrs Pym

Words fail me to express my enjoyment of *Excellent Women*, but I must try to say something because it would be a pity if you did not know what *immense* pleasure you have given to me – and doubtless to countless others too...For 17 years I was in the category of 'excellent women' myself and except that my 'excellence' functioned in a village instead of town parish, my experience, thoughts and emotions were so exactly like Mildred's that you might have been writing about me...I simply loved the book, and think it the best novel I have ever read...

A reader from New Zealand wrote:

Thank you very much indeed for many pleasant hours and quiet chuckles. After reading *Excellent Women* I made a special trip to our nearest library for *Some Tame Gazelle* which I have just finished, with even more enjoyment...I shall be looking forward to announcements of any further writing from your witty pen, which is never really unkind...

However, there is usually one reader it is impossible to satisfy. This letter from 31 Palace Road, Llandaff is undated, without salutation, and unsigned.

Mrs Macintosh enjoyed reading *Excellent Women* but she writes to say that it was spoilt for her by touches of vulgarity – who does it please to talk about Ladies' Rooms and sanitary paper? Certainly not the people who would enjoy EW. Mrs Macintosh quickly decided not to buy the book.

I am surprised that she did not include among the vulgar touches the 'unpleasantness' that was dropped into Mrs Bone's lap by a passing bird!

After years of discussion with members of the Barbara Pym Society, if I were asked which of her novels was first favourite among them I would suggest *Excellent Women*. Taking the long view several years after Barbara's death, Robert Liddell[1] concluded that *Excellent Women* 'is, I think, the best novel in the 'canon'(his word for the first six novels), and Robert Emmet Long[2] considered it 'exceptional in its originality...it is one of the most distinctive comic novels to have appeared in England since World War II'.

7

Jane and Prudence:
A Novel of Contrasts

1950 – 1954

Jane and Prudence, friends from Oxford days,
may be said to represent the married
and the unmarried, the country
and the town…Neither woman is entirely
successful in her life.

Jane and Prudence: *A Novel of Contrasts*

The Bodleian archive consists of literary papers and notebooks, diaries, and correspondence, and over the years I have been able to extract from these a good deal of material. Along with examining partial and complete drafts of the novels, much of my research has focused on Barbara's literary notebooks, which she kept from 1948 until shortly before her death – 43 in all. They contain all sorts of jottings; many are ideas for possible novels, but sometimes she wrote accounts of holidays, extracts from some book she had read, or a poem she had found. Always there are lists at the back – shopping lists, Christmas card lists, details of her winter or summer wardrobe, and lists of books she had read during the period.

However, when starting to research this chapter, I found the only entry for *Jane and Prudence* in the index to the Bodleian manuscripts is 'Correspondence relating to the novel and radio broadcast'. Without drafts I could not at first see how I could proceed, but the contents of the literary notebooks are not analysed in the index, so there was a chance that I could find something there.

There are indeed fairly extensive notes for *Jane and Prudence* in the notebooks covering 1950-1953. They are largely about characters and events which eventually appear in the book; unlike the notes for some of her novels, there is little which was later discarded. She seems to have had a rather clear idea of her plot before she started.

In a summary of *Jane and Prudence* that Barbara later wrote as a publisher's blurb, she said,

> Jane and Prudence, friends from Oxford days, may be said to represent the married and the unmarried, the country and the town. Two contrasting environments are shown – the country village where Jane's husband is vicar, and that part of London

where Prudence works at her rather indefinite job. Village and office provide a variety of characters. Prudence works for the ineffectual Dr Grampian and with that irritating pair Miss Trapnell and Miss Clothier, while Jane, with her vague and charming husband, becomes involved in the lives of Miss Doggett and her poor relation Jessie Morrow, and the affected Fabian Driver, who fancies himself in the role of an inconsolable widower.

It is Jane who provides the link between the two worlds, both by her friendship with Prudence and by her strong sense of the ridiculous which helps her to see people with a certain amount of detachment, for neither woman is entirely successful in her life. Prudence romanticises herself and her love affairs, which do not seem to be very successful ones, while Jane imagines herself as an efficient vicar's wife and the provider of a suitable husband for her friend. But things do not turn out quite the way she had hoped. Church people in the country are no easier to deal with than those in the suburbs, and eligible men are not always willing to have their lives arranged for them.

Hazel Holt wrote that 'Jane Cleveland is a loving celebration of Irena Pym (with academic overtones),' but I don't feel that this really does Barbara's mother justice. Admittedly she was a little careless in her dress, was unable to draw or paint, and never learnt to sew, but she did most of the family cooking, fed the chickens (wearing an old tweed coat like Jane's), looked after Mogus the pony who pulled the governess cart that she drove, was usually the car driver, rather than her husband, and she herself also rode a motor cycle, even as far as Pwelheli, a journey of over 70 miles. She was also musical and athletic, being good at most games, especially golf.

Jane, on the other hand, has singularly few abilities, housewifely or otherwise. 'You know how indifferent I am to domestic arrangements,' she says, and the kitchen was a part of the house in which she took little interest. She does confess that she 'should have liked the kind of life where one ate food flavoured with garlic, but it was not to be.' She simply is not sufficiently interested in cooking. The only kitchen utensil with which she is familiar is the tin-opener, her washing-up method leaves much to be desired, and her husband can rarely find a clean shirt. She even pours tea badly. 'The ability to pour tea gracefully didn't come to me automatically when I married.'

Jane also concedes that she is no good at parish work – she can't arrange flowers, or interest herself much to the Mothers' Union, and lacks tact at the Parochial Church Council meetings. Even when she decides to resume her abandoned literary studies, she soon gets bored. It is a bit difficult to find anything she *is* good at. In spite of this, she comes across as a lovable and sympathetic character, and in this one aspect surely resembles Irena.

Hazel Holt also tells us that Prudence, with her predilection for unsatisfactory love affairs, is only a slightly distorted mirror image of Barbara herself, and Barbara herself used to say that of all her heroines, in many ways the one she resembled most was Prudence. She also told Philip Larkin that Prudence and Wilmet from *A Glass of Blessings* were her own favourite characters.

Barbara's notes are just that – odd jottings, often poorly punctuated, sometimes almost illegible, so never easy to follow. It is not always clear what is fact and what fiction. Her first entry on the subject after the completion of *Excellent Women* is:

> Next Novel – a small country town – perhaps the chief character a nice vicar's wife. Her husband is the son of an old Rationalist – he had probably probed too deeply and got suddenly and disconcertedly at the truth. A daughter preparing the house for the bank clerk lay reader, with whom she is in love, to come to tea. But surely he won't want a bath. The wife sits on committees. Is literary, but no time for that now – perhaps had even wanted to do research ('The influence of Somebody on Something'). Missed opportunities. Jane felt she has not been really successful – but a happy marriage and a child, people might say rather reproachfully, wasn't that something?
>
> The wife has a sister (unmarried) who lives in a flat in London and has a career. It is taken for granted that she has always been in love with a certain man.

The novel, she says firmly, contrasts the married and the unmarried.

Of the village characters, the first Barbara mentions is Fabian Driver, and sums up in few words 'his Gordonish character.' Gordon Glover was, of course, Barbara's real-life lover in Bristol in the early 1940s, an extremely charming but fickle man who caused Barbara much heartache. However, apparently Gordon was 'intellectually far above' Fabian, and had none of the vulgarity which Robert Liddell so rightly finds in him.

> Fabian's wife, to whom he had been consistently unfaithful, died – now that he has lost her there seems to be no point in being unfaithful. He visits her grave frequently, and although he has work it doesn't seem to require his attendance every day of the week.

In a passage which also sums up Jane – her appearance anyway – she writes,

> Fabian liked Jane really – but it was an insult, an outrage almost, how unconscious she was of his charm, how little effort she made with her clothes – galoshes, old mackintosh, shapeless hat, the strap of her sandal pinned with a safety pin. But she feels the same about him – in his overcoat on a fine spring day – probably woollen underwear too.

Next Barbara introduces some minor characters, including Mr Mortlake, piano tuner and member of the Parochial Church Council (PCC):

> Oh dear, I'm humming again, she thought, recognising a nervous habit that kind friends had often pointed out to her. Something from *Rigoletto* – suitable for Mr. Mortlake or not? Perhaps too violent – she wanted to gesticulate, bowing low and saying 'Buon giorno, Rigoletto' with the irony of the mocking courtiers. Then, in her relief at finding that he has only come to tune the piano, she puts on his bowler and sings *O Donna Clara*.

In fact, this is exactly what her mother had done on one occasion Barbara remembered when their piano tuner, Mr Passmore, had called.

Next, Mr Whiting, also on the PCC, who resembles 'Some old fish with his tail stuck in his mouth.' If there is one thing generally known about this otherwise unremarkable fish, it is that whiting is served with its tail in its mouth. Mrs Beeton's recipe for fried whiting states 'Wash, clean, and dry the fish, and remove their skins, and fasten the tail in the mouth by means of a small skewer.'

Mrs Glaze gets a mention.

> In the old days, thought Jane, one asked of a servant 'Is she a good riser?' It would be impertinent to think of Mrs. Glaze as being capable of such ordinary occupations as going to bed and getting up – impertinent even to think of her without her hat and flowered apron. She had 'done' for the last vicar – a formidable interview Jane has had with her – she was always talking about the old days and the entertaining.

The Lyalls do not appear in the notes, though they are thought to be based on Julian Amery and his mother.

The far more important village characters, Miss Doggett and Miss Morrow, are never formally introduced, probably because Barbara had them firmly in her mind as they had already appeared in an earlier novel, *Crampton Hodnet,* as yet unpublished. They are briefly mentioned in the notes, where we first encounter Miss Doggett's timeless words 'Men only want one thing.'

Of the London characters, Barbara decided that the main one should be a friend of Jane's rather than a sister:

> The clergyman's wife has an old college friend, Prudence, who works in London (at a place like the International African Institute). She is in love with her boss. All her love affairs are unrequited. The surprise when Jane sees the object of Prudence's affections – a grey-haired man, quite insignificant.
>
> Her boss, Dr Grampian, an economist, has a wife Lucy and children, Susan and Barnabas. Prudence had once had the idea of fidelity as a very fine thing. Loving a person always, but if they changed, where were you? Then faithfulness became a chilly, dreary thing…Like a great renunciation for the wrong

reasons. She might have a great renunciation with Gramp, making it much more noble than it really is, and he not understanding. 'Ah, Prudence,' he had once said, laying his hand on hers, perhaps even kissing her. Whatever had made him do it? There had been Lucy at home as usual. 'Rather late tonight dear, aren't you?' so mildly, and then talking of other things.

Incidentally, there is no suggestion that that Grampian, Director of the 'vague cultural organisation' where Prudence worked, is at all like Daryll Forde, Barbara's boss at the IAI, who was a far more forceful and decisive man. Hazel Holt thinks that Grampian is 'too grey and nebulous a creature to bear any resemblance to him.'

At this point, Barbara considers the possibility that Prudence might end up with the Gordon man (Fabian).

> There is another man on the staff [Mr. Manifold] – the only one except for Gramp. He goes furtively to his lunch – perhaps to a pub or more manly place. But one day our heroine sees him in the queue of Lyons' Help Yourself. The mantle falls. She averts her eyes.

> In the office Miss Trapnell and Miss Clothier in their shrunken cardigans, specially kept for the office. But when did they blossom out in their best clothes?

> Mr. Manifold and the typists discuss Prudence. 'Do you suppose Miss Bates has any love life?'

Both Prudence in the country and Jane in the town often find themselves uncomfortably out of place.

> The single woman finds the vicarage bare and untidy, comfortless and noisy, and is so much more at home with her uncomfortable but very pretty little Regency sofa, planning a dinner by candlelight, exquisitely cooked, perhaps by herself in a velvet dress with antique garnet jewellery.

Jane looks forward to her visits to London, though she often finds them vaguely disappointing, and sometimes feels at a loss, as when she was too early for her lunch appointment with Prudence, and wanders into the unaccustomed luxury of Fortnum and Mason's, where she stares at some jars of *foie gras*, something a clergyman's wife could never afford.

She is, however, slightly more at ease at a Literary Society in London, 'where she sees people like herself talking together and then going off afterwards – alone – to the bus, the underground, the taxi … She finds herself interested in one, a tall woman with prominent teeth, nervous looking – her book "Some Tame something".' This oblique reference to Barbara the writer is omitted in the novel. You may remember that she used a similar device at the Anchorage Hotel in *No Fond Return of Love*.

Having decided upon her characters, Barbara considers her plot, and gives herself some instructions on how to proceed.

> At the beginning you must describe how Jane had imagined her life as a clergyman's wife and how it had turned out in reality. Well, it has all turned to mild kindly looks and spectacles – he put them on to eat now, to dissect kippers – and perhaps being a clergyman didn't really make any difference – it would have been the same in the Senior Common Room at the London School of Economics…His large nose was more pronounced now.

Other 'things to be brought out', as Barbara puts it, are:

> 1) Prudence's mother in Herefordshire [who ultimately gets only a passing mention]
>
> 2) Prudence ought to have more women friends in London – ones upon whom she can fall back when Fabian has abandoned her. [However, it was a man, Mr Manifold, whom she chiefly fell back upon.]
>
> 3) Her women friends. Especially Eleanor, the dull civil servant. [In the end there was only Eleanor, and she wasn't all that dull.]
>
> 4) The relationship between Jane and Prudence and their respective ages.
>
> 5) The end of Prudence – sitting in a railway carriage on her way to Spain, reading Coventry Patmore. And the man thinks 'Who is that interesting-looking woman reading Coventry Patmore? [In the finished novel, this happens far less romanti-

cally, over lunch in a cheap restaurant.]

6) Read some of Miss Austen's last chapters and find out how she manages all the loose ends.

Now for the two characters who sprang into *Jane and Prudence* almost fully formed – Miss Doggett and Miss Morrow. These are among the main characters in *Crampton Hodnet*, chronologically Barbara's second full-length novel, written in 1938-9, but unpublished until after her death. When reviewing her writings after the war, Barbara decided that *Crampton Hodnet* was very dated, and would not be acceptable to a publisher, so she put it aside. But Barbara never liked to waste any of her work, so she must have considered that these two ladies would fit well into the country aspect of *Jane and Prudence*. They appear to be about the same age in both novels, and in both Miss Doggett is dressed in purple with gold neck chains. But it is interesting to see the changes Barbara made to their personalities. In *Crampton Hodnet* Miss Doggett is more dictatorial generally, and very dismissive of her companion's appearance and opinions. In *Jane and Prudence* she seems to have mellowed just a little and to be slightly less inclined to browbeat Jessie. This may be because in this book Jessie is her kinswoman, and therefore requiring a little more respect, so much so that when Jessie finally finds a husband, Miss Doggett is keen to support her.

Miss Morrow has developed from the very put-upon employee of *Crampton Hodnet*, grateful to have a comfortable home even though her job is menial, to a more assertive woman. She is more scheming and self-seeking than heretofore, and rather more inclined to speak openly. It would be difficult to imagine the Jessie of *Crampton Hodnet* saying, when discussing a woman's right to wear a white wedding dress after the age of thirty. 'There can be something shameful about flaunting one's lack of experience.'

Another important character from *Crampton Hodnet* who also appears in *Jane and Prudence*, though in a minor role, is Barbara Bird. Barbara has aged rather more quickly than Miss Doggett and Miss Morrow. In *Crampton Hodnet* she is a dewy-eyed undergraduate romantically in love with her tutor; ten or so years on, her abortive elopement with Francis

Cleveland seems to have driven romance, and the metaphysical poets, from her life, to be replaced by heavy smoking, dog ownership, and seventeen published novels. 'Miss Bird's readers know what to expect now, and they will not be disappointed.'

It is amusing to meet again Dora's brother from *Excellent Women*, for indeed it is William Caldicote, that *bon viveur*, who gives unsolicited advice to Prudence and Geoffrey Manifold in a Soho restaurant: 'I do *not* recommend the pâté here tonight, but the bouillabaisse is excellent.' And we hear that Miss Lathbury from that same novel has indeed married Everard Bone.

On 18 February 1953 Barbara wrote to Daniel George at Cape's,

> Dear Daniel
>
> Tomorrow I shall be posting the manuscript of my novel *Jane and Prudence* to you…I hope you are not too much all agog to see it or you will surely be disappointed…Naturally it has not turned out quite as I had hoped. I had wanted the contrasting lives of Jane and Prudence, in town and country, to stand out more. As it is they are perhaps just two rather tiresome and unsuccessful women, though there is hope for them in the end. I hope you will not find Chapter 12 too shocking…

This is the chapter in which Jane quizzes Prudence about her relationship with Fabian. '"I suppose everything is all right between you and Fabian? I mean, there's nothing wrong between you?" Jane laboured, using an expression she had sometimes seen in the cheaper women's papers when girls asked how they should behave when their boy-friends wanted them to "do wrong".'

Daniel replied a week later

> I've now recovered *Jane and Prudence* and am enjoying it enormously. But (just between ourselves) don't you think that far too many lines of dialogue begin with 'Oh', 'Oh dear', or 'Oh well'? Please look at your carbon copy and steel yourself to sacrifice some of them.

On 4 March, Daniel wrote again:

I refrained from saying anything about your novel when we met, but I can now announce that William Plomer is as pleased with it as I am. [William Plomer, the South African novelist, was literary adviser to Cape at that time.]

Very shortly after publication in September, Barbara received a bombshell in the form of a letter from the Legal Department of Marks and Spencer's:

> It has been brought to our notice that on p. 125 of the edition of the novel *Jane and Prudence* there appears a reference to this Company in the following terms:
>
> 'I am going to send most of these things to the Society for the Care of Aged Gentlewomen', said Miss Doggett. 'Not that Constance was aged herself, but one does feel that they need good clothes, the elderly ones.' 'Oh, yes,' Jane agreed; 'when we become distressed we shall be glad of an old dress from Marks and Spencer's as we've never been used to anything better.' Miss Doggett did not answer, and Jane remembered that of course she went to her dressmaker for fittings and ordered hats from Marshall's and Debenham's'.
>
> This reference is clearly derogatory of the Company as both in terms and by implication it suggests that dresses sold by this Company are of inferior quality and unfit for wear by persons of the class who buy their hats from Marshall's or Debenham's.
>
> We are proud of the quality of the goods sold by us, and take great exception to this passage in a book which, being a Book Society's recommendation, and being written by an author whose work, according to the Publisher's 'blurb' on the dustcover, is at times 'worthy of Jane Austen', no doubt enjoys a large circulation.
>
> We must therefore ask you to inform us at once what steps you propose to take to correct the harm done by the publication of this matter and to prevent further publication.

Wren Howard, a director at Cape, advised Barbara not to reply to this 'somewhat threatening letter' and said that he would consult his solicitors. They pointed out to M&S that the allusion referred to was not derogatory of their goods.

We suggest that if you will reconsider the passage in the light of the general atmosphere and characterisation of Miss Pym's novel, you will appreciate an ironical note underlying the dialogue and the implication of snobbishness by Miss Doggett, arising precisely out of the fact that the name of your firm is a 'household word' for goods remarkable no less for their inexpensiveness than for their high quality.

He added in a PS, that he had received a letter from Miss Barbara Pym, in which she says:-

I need hardly tell you that I certainly never intended anything derogatory to Marks and Spencer's, for whom I have the greatest respect. The ironical thing is that I regularly buy and wear their clothes and think them excellent.

However, M&S would not accept Cape's interpretation and pressed for 'adequate action to be taken to ensure that this reference to our name is cut out of copies of the book placed before the public in future'.

Cape agreed to alter the passage in future printings. Barbara's amendment was thus:

'Oh, yes', Jane agreed; 'When we become distressed we shan't expect to receive anything very grand, considering the sort of clothes we're wearing now.'
I hope this will do. If you think that Marshall's and Debenham's should be taken out too, we could substitute 'expensive shops in London.'

M&S next complained that a reprint still included the offending words, but Wren Howard explained that this reprint had been ordered before M&S's first letter:

I was finally compelled, as I feared, to cause our solicitor to write to these tiresome people and attempt to quieten them. I am glad now to report that he has today received a letter saying that, in view of the information we have supplied, and an undertaking to change the passage in any reprint, they are pacified and pleased to accept our assurance that nothing derogatory to them was ever intended. I hope the matter is thus ended and that all is well.

Personally, I think that M&S had a good case against Cape, and am surprised that they caved in without much of a struggle. The odd thing is that there is no evidence that the passage was ever changed in any subsequent editions – certainly it is unchanged in the 1993 Pan edition which I have been using. Nor is it omitted from the American or recent Virago editions.

On 16 September Barbara received another interesting letter which I should have thought she would have found very exciting. It was from Derrick de Marney, a well-known British actor of that time, and director of a company called Concanen Stage Plays.

> Dear Miss Pym,
>
> I have just read your new book *Jane and Prudence* which has deeply interested me. Primarily the reason is that I feel that you understand post-war human beings.
>
> Have you by any chance considered this new subject in play form? Your dialogue suggests that you may have some experience of writing for the theatre. If you have not considered a play on this subject, have you in play form, any stories which you would permit me to read?
>
> Although my name has been associated for so long with the successful production of Peter Cheyney's 'Meet Mr Callaghan,' I do not particularly want anything of the thriller or detective type. I am looking for any subject dealing with post-war problems.
>
> Forgive me for writing to you so abruptly, but I know of no other way in which I can approach you. I do sincerely congratulate you upon your new publication, which I have thoroughly enjoyed in book form, and am looking forward to hearing from you.

Amazingly, there is no follow-up to this among Barbara's papers. One would have thought that she would have jumped at the opportunity.

Barbara's friends were quick to congratulate her. An anthropologist friend from Philadelphia, H. D. Gunn, wrote on behalf of himself and his wife Virginia:

> We've had *Jane and Prudence*, the dears!…We think you're getting beautifully into stride, now…I had really only one rather small criticism, or rather comment, to make. It seems to me… well, this character Manifold is a fine type, but somehow I had the feeling all along that you weren't making the most of him, that he had unused depth…a kind of potential nobility that you should have exploited to the advantage of your scheme as a whole.

A clergyman friend, Fr Luxmoore Ball, wrote from Hastings, Sussex:

> In my opinion this is your best book so far. If you asked me why I think that I would say because there is more action and incidents in this story, more variety in the characters, and their 'fun' is more 'human.'

And a friend at the British Consulate in Florence, writing on 19 December 1953, said:

> I am writing on the spur of the moment having just put down 'J&P.' I think it is excellent – I like it better than *Excellent Women*, though most people I've met do not agree. The characters seem so much more real – Prudence particularly. I feel as though I've seen something very clear and polished; no disturbance of details; nothing that takes your mind from the whole. I am left with a positive feeling as though I had 'caught' some of the clarity, seen life as a whole again. Surely this is the test of a work of art. I did not have this feeling after EW.

Another friend, Jean Telford, wrote from Paris:

> I enjoyed it even more than your other books. I keep repeating bits to myself on the Métro, things like 'Just the very best, that is what a man needs,' and then smiling, and all those cold clear intelligent French faces look at me pretty sharply…

Catherine Goodacre, a fan from Reading, Berkshire, wrote to say:

> It was with such a feeling of sadness and loss that I took back to the library today J&P, which has held me enthralled literally from beginning to end…I can't pretend to compete with the

critics, who with their professional understanding of the perfection of your own particular style of writing, have praised your work. All I can say is that through your novels I have experienced a joy only comparable with that which came to me at the age of 14 or so when I first 'discovered' Jane Austen.

In a letter to Bob Smith dated 22 April 1954, Barbara says:

> I had a letter from Jock recently. He liked J&P very much. [He found it 'so witty, kind and sharp.'] But the Americans and Continentals most definitely don't and now I am feeling a little bruised.

Hazel Holt notes in *A Lot To Ask* that it 'was a Book Society Recommendation, and was well received, though some critics were uncertain about the more flexible structure.'

In fact, *The Observer* found the book 'too loose and rambling not to disappoint after *Excellent Women*.' The *Manchester Guardian* was quite hostile:

> It is a horrid disappointment after *Excellent Women*. God and the Devil would never make over even the smallest English village, let alone suburb, to a set of miseducated nincompoops like the people in this tale.

The *TLS* wrote, 'more in sorrow than in anger' as Hazel put it,

> Some incidents occur; they are not easy to recall after one has closed the book. Miss Pym writes very well, and this chronicle of [Jane's] doings is really very small beer indeed to have come from a brewery in which Oxford, a taste for Jane Austen, and an observant eye have all played their parts.

But the *News Chronicle* found it 'a brilliant and charming novel, which you will not easily forget', and Lord David Cecil, in the first of a number of letters he wrote to Barbara, said:

> Forgive a total stranger writing to tell you how very much he enjoys your books…You have so much sense of reality and sense of comedy, and the people in your books are living and credible and likeable. I find this rare in modern fiction. Thank

you very much.

The only American review I found was by Stephen Harvey in *The Village Voice* in December 1981, when it was first published in the US.

> J&P is a nearly perfect specimen of the lapidary fiction which can reveal more about the essence of things than can books with big thumping ambitions. Pym's subject may be outmoded, but her observations of homely human detail are as potent as ever.

Several times in her notes and diary, Barbara expressed dissatisfaction with this novel. She felt she had not emphasised the contrasts between country and town, and the married and unmarried states, as clearly as she had wished. And she thought it was 'ill-fated, what with the M&S business, and it wasn't really very good anyway, though a surprising number of people like it better than *Excellent Women.'* Perhaps that is why she did not leave behind much evidence of the development of this novel.

By 1955 *Jane and Prudence* was out of print. It was not reissued until 1978, when Barbara's reputation was rising again, and all her work was about to be reappraised – and indeed to be as highly praised as it deserved.

An earlier version of this paper was presented at the 2012 North American Conference in Cambridge, Massachusetts.

8

Less Than Angels:
A Look at the Background of the 'Anthropological Novel'

1952 – 1958

After the war, I got a job at the International
African Institute in London…I learned
how it was possible and even essential to cultivate an
attitude of detachment towards life
and people, and how the novelist could even do
'field-work' as the anthropologist did.

Less Than Angels: *A Look at the Background of the 'Anthropological Novel'*

In May 1978 Barbara Pym gave a talk to the Senior Wives Fellowship of Oxford University entitled *The Ups and Downs of a Writer's Life*. In it she said,

> My work at the International African Institute, where I was in daily contact with anthropologists and their work, was indirectly useful to me as a novelist. The anthropologist goes out into the field to study so-called 'primitive' societies, and to note their customs. Coming nearer home, this technique can very well be applied to our own society, to the things that go on in our everyday life. My novel *Less Than Angels* is the one that shows this most clearly, but I have been influenced by the anthropologists in other ways – I think especially by looking at fictional situations with scientific detachment – but I hope also with sympathy.[1]

The techniques used by anthropologists – observation, notation and deduction – were employed by Barbara too.

Her idea of writing a novel set in an anthropological research institute seems to have arisen in the early 1950s. Barbara always carried with her a little notebook in which she jotted down her thoughts on any projects she was working on at the time, or any idea that struck her as interesting or amusing that could perhaps be used later, and entries for *Less Than Angels* can be found throughout the notebooks covering the years 1952-1955. Many of these are general, like possible names for her characters – Gervase, Martin, Felix, Cyril for the men, Primrose, Vanessa, Deirdre, Deborah for the women – and thoughts on the opening chapter: 'A possible beginning – the young man coming back from Africa – to his provincial (or suburban) mother and her bridge-playing friends.

Or begin with the funeral of a venerable anthropologist.'

There is also among Barbara's papers a 36-leaved booklet, dating from April 1953, devoted entirely to *Less Than Angels*. This is a handsome collection of more or less disjointed paragraphs, some fairly lengthy, and some which appear almost unchanged in the novel, but it can in no way be considered a compete draft.

The character of Tom Mallow, rather than any of the others, was the starting point for *Less Than Angels* – even his name was in no doubt from the beginning. In her notebook for 1952-3 her first words relating to this novel are 'The young hero of the anthropological novel has many woman friends and admirers, but chooses none. He might refer to them callously as his girl friends – perhaps Africa or its people are his real love?'

While other aspects of the book underwent revision, this theme remained unchanged. Barbara's notes describe Tom as 'in no way remarkable to look at – of only medium height, rather too thin with dark brown hair.' But in the definitive version he was made rather more attractive: 'He was tall and dark, with thin aristocratic features, and brilliant grey eyes.' Barbara also wanted it made quite clear from the outset that Tom was a brilliant anthropologist, and that 'although beloved of several women, his main interest was always in his work.' When Tom was thinking about Deirdre, the truth suddenly came to him.

> He realized with a mixture of apprehension, gratification and astonishment that it was not his tribe she was interested in, but him. Land tenure, age sets, kinship terminology – could it be that all these meant nothing to her?

When Deirdre 'imagines him seething with all kinds of passions, really he is just quietly at home reading or writing his thesis,' or even 'going to Watford to talk about the lineage system' – Watford, where the bracing air was hoped to revive him after his return from Africa 'looking so terribly "White Man's Grave".' In the following year's notebook Barbara decided on Tom's death, a drastic move, and one unprecedented n the Pym novels. 'Tom died doing something rather secret, political and splendid. Oh, dear, is he going to be a kind of Lawrence of Arabia? He dies the kind of death one of his class might have died in, say 1907.'

Barbara then considered her heroines. Strangely, there is no direct reference to Catherine in the notebooks – her name and occupation are never mentioned, nor any details of her relationship with Tom. However, Barbara must have had a triangular situation in mind, because quite early on she notes, 'The two women who love the young anthropologist must meet together.' It must be Catherine, now in her early thirties, to whom Barbara is referring when she says, 'Perhaps the young woman who loves an anthropologist can have been a Wren officer, aged 20, at Westcliff-on-Sea or in the New Forest before the invasion.'

As for Deirdre, 'I think the girl meets the young anthropologist at a party…' Note that Catherine is *the young woman* but Deirdre is *the girl.* 'Can the girl who loves him work in a library and get books for him?' In the booklet, Deirdre is an English graduate from Oxford, now working as an assistant librarian at Felix's research centre. 'On coming down from Oxford she had hoped to marry a Great Love, but she had not yet found one.' Eventually, however, Deirdre becomes an anthropology student at the University of London 'rather than a husband-hunting Oxford graduate'.

Barbara considers other characters in her notes, some of whom are preserved after modification. Felix Byron Mainwaring appears early on as 'an aging Professor of Anthropology who is still attractive to women – has perhaps had several wives – and feels the burden of his middle name!' And the Lydgates: ' I think there could be a missionary brother (she a linguist) living in a cluttered suburban or country house full of African relics. They live with their old father – a Rationalist – who is grieved at the idea of his son's being a clergyman.' The idea of Lydgate as a clergyman persists in the booklet. He had a parish in Oxford, and it was through him that Deirdre was introduced to his sister and Miss Clovis. He was, moreover, a deeply unhappy man. 'His work in Africa had not brought a stream of converts to the mission, he had achieved nothing in the field of anthropology or linguistics, he was not even a good parish priest and knew himself to be disliked by most of his congregation… In one field he had achieved some fame or notoriety – he was well known as a writer of vitriolic reviews.'

That last bit, at least, was preserved. Other ideas were considered, then discarded. 'Ought not Theo Grote (Theodore Mbawawa) and his wife Constance come in somewhere?' and 'You must have parrot's eggs in somewhere – Alaric Lydgate and Tom [as the sender and recipient, presumably] – perhaps the Dulke's have a parrot who lays an egg….'

These notes provide only tenuous links to the finished novel. There must have been many intermediate drafts which have not survived.

On 10 October 1954 Barbara noted,

> Today finished my fourth novel, about an anthropologist (no title as yet).
>
> Typed from 10.30 am to 3.30 pm sustained by, in the following order, a cup of milky Nescafe, a gin and French, cold beef, baked potato, tomato and grated cheese, rice pudding and plums.

However, another five months passed before Barbara sent the completed novel to Daniel George at Cape.

On 4 April 1955 Jonathan Cape wrote, 'I have read *Less Than Angels* with great satisfaction. It is very good and very charming I think. I have pleasure in sending you a contract…' She received an advance of £100, and a few days later, '…we will certainly try hard to place *Less Than Angels* with an American publisher. American publishers are funny people. They seem to be less and less addicted to English books, and they have a raw bright attitude, thinking not that a book is good but whether it will *sell* well. For my part, I have never known when a book would sell. I try to go for what I think is good.' Daniel George added, 'I think you've achieved something as near perfection as it could be, and I have great hopes for its popular and esteemed success.'

An unfortunate blip occurred just before publication. Jenifer Armstrong, Cape's Advertising Manager, wrote to Barbara to apologise for putting 'ornithologists' instead of 'anthropologists' in her publicity advertisement in *The Listener*: '…there is no excuse, as I have read your book and enjoyed it very much, but I shall naturally see that in future it reads "anthropologists," and apologise again.'

The book was published at 13/6 (about 70p) on 17 October 1955. The first to congratulate her was her friend Frances Atkin:

> Dearest Buddy, I must write to you at once to tell you how tremendously I have enjoyed *Less Than Angels* which I have devoured with almost indecent greed. I think it is far and away your best, more subtly shrewd, penetrating and funny even than *Excellent Women*. It is a complete triumph in every way...I hope it will have the resounding success it deserves.

And the next was Robert Liddell:

> Dearest Barbara,
>
> Thank you very much indeed for your book, which delighted me.
>
> Anthropologists have something of the comforting charm of Bodleian readers, and I feel at home with them – the glimpses of church were tantalising, however. Do give us more and stronger incense next time. I very much liked the visit to the country house...Ivy, Elizabeth and Olivia all think poorly of *Anglo-Saxon Attitudes* – I am sure it is not so nice as *Less Than Angels*.

These were of course the novelists Ivy Compton-Burnett, Elizabeth Taylor, and Olivia Manning, ganging up on poor Angus Wilson!

A slightly sour note was introduced only a few days after publication. Despite Jonathan Cape's assertion that he only went for 'good' books, rather than those that sell, his partner, the verbose Wren Howard, was reviewing the pre-publication sales figures.

> I have only just woken up to the fact that I omitted to write to you before publication of *Less Than Angels*...The reason for this was that I wanted to compare the number of the present novel sold before publication with similar figures for *Jane and Prudence*. I had a slightly uneasy feeling that subscription figures for the new novel were not quite so good as those for the earlier one and I am afraid that I was right. We subscribed about 2050

for *Less Than Angels*, which in general isn't a bad figure, but does not compare too favourably with the 2300 subscription to *Jane and Prudence*. I cannot rightly explain this slight decline, but imagine it is not unconnected with the collapse and bankruptcy of the large wholesale booksellers, Simpkin Marshall, from whom we might have expected a substantial order for a novel such as yours.

However, more praise from her friends. 'No. 4 [i.e. Pym's fourth novel] is having a great success with the Barnicots and their friends,' writes Elizabeth. 'Also, I believe, in the British Council. Mary [Hare] and I were particularly struck by your understanding of the YOUNG and your sympathy with them. I especially liked Mark and Digby, not only because they are so well-drawn, but because of their chorus-like part in the story.' And from an unknown fan, 'May I express my enormous pleasure in your books, particularly in the one I have just finished, *Less Than Angels*…This is my favourite, followed by *Jane and Prudence*, *Excellent Women*, and *Some Tame Gazelle* in that order…I hope you will not consider it an impertinence when I say that I consider your books by far the best of their genre in recent years.'

Peggy Makins, better known as Evelyn Home, who answered readers' problem letters in *Women's Own* magazine, wrote:

> Thank you very much for *Less Than Angels* – contrary to some critics, I find little acid in your work, although it is invariably dressed with a sharp sauce…May I criticise a mere point of fact? As a journalist (working for a women's magazine) I am sure Catherine would never have been permitted to suggest remedies like lemon rind and cucumber skin. Beauty writers work under the whiplash of Advertising Departments. Catherine would have written of a certain skinfood which was death to wrinkled elbows. But this is mere carping. It is a lovely book, and almost long enough.

The novelist Elizabeth Taylor, with whom Barbara had been corresponding fairly regularly, also wrote to her. Unfortunately the letter is undated, and does not even mention the title of the book she is writing about, but I think it must have been *Less Than Angels*.

Dear Barbara,

It was such a nice surprise to get your book and kind of you to send it. Now I have read it and was sorry to finish it. I wished that it would last longer. I think that I liked it the best of all – yes, I'm sure that I did. It is always interesting to get a glimpse of other circles. I am alarmed when I find myself among learned, academic people, who talk about their theses…and enjoyed finding out about their failings, and that they can often be childish…I should have liked more of that pleasant suburbia, so well described and easily imagined. I always feel I know what you are writing about and that, either from my own experience or through you, I know it too.

Towards the end of the year, Wren Howard was on to her again about sales figures:

Total sales up to the end of last week amount to 3092 copies, which isn't good enough, but that certainly isn't your fault – what the book now requires is an advertisement of some kind or another through the BBC. Cannot you contrive to have it read in 'Woman's Hour'? That would make all the difference.

In August 1956 Cape wrote,

I am sure you will be pleased to learn that *Less Than Angels* is to appear in the USA. You'll have lovely reviews, even if you don't sell any. Americans do review so nicely.

The book was published in the United States on 1 April 1957. On the same day, Jacques Chambrun, a New York agent, wrote,

I have just finished *Less Than Angels*, and I want to congratulate you on a book that gives the reader an uncommonly vivid experience. It is sustained, consistent, and well-balanced, and it leads us to hope that you have time for, or possibly have on hand, shorter work that could be offered for magazine publication.

Despite his personal enthusiasm, Chambrun was unable to place her short stories.

By March 1958 the total number of copies of *Less Than Angels* sold in the United States was 1386. 'I still do not seem to have earned my $500 advance,' recorded Barbara sadly.

I could find no newspaper reviews of this book among Barbara's papers, but the inference is that the critics were not as greatly impressed as they had been with, say, *Excellent Women*. Since sales were relatively poor, though this was largely due to the closing of the subscription libraries, and the demise of Simpkin Marshall, and probably poor marketing, perhaps her readers were not too keen either, possibly because of the unfamiliarity of the setting. Barbara herself said, in a talk at Barnes in the 1950s, 'I suppose readers can be divided into two classes – those who like a setting that is familiar to them or that they can imagine without too much difficulty, and the others who want to be taken right out of their everyday lives and dumped down…in a setting that they wouldn't normally find themselves in.'

Perhaps Barbara's loyal readers belonged in the first category, and preferred the familiar world of the village, the vicarage, and the jumble sale.

An earlier version of this paper was presented at the 2003 Annual General Meeting in Oxford.

9

'WHAT IS MY NEXT NOVEL TO BE?'

The Lime Tree Bower,
afterwards called A Glass of Blessings

1955 – 1958

It can begin with the shrilling of the telephone bell
in Freddie Hood's church, and end with
a flame springing up on Easter Saturday in the dark
church…But what about the middle?

'WHAT IS MY NEXT NOVEL TO BE?'

On Sunday 10 October 1954 Barbara Pym wrote in her notebook 'Today finished my fourth novel about the anthropologists.' This, of course, was *Less Than Angels*, published a few months later.

Having had three well-reviewed novels published in the previous four years, Barbara embarked on her fifth with no misgivings about its acceptance by her publisher, but also with no clear idea of a subject. She must have thought about it for quite some time, for it was not until May of the following year (1955) that she wrote in her notebook, in capital letters, 'WHAT IS MY NEXT NOVEL TO BE?'

She answers her own question thus: 'It can begin with the shrilling of the telephone bell in Freddie Hood's church, and end with a flame springing up on Easter Saturday in the dark church...But what about the middle?'

The Reverend Frederick Hood, a canon of St Paul's, who had been the principal of Pusey House, the Anglican Centre in Oxford, from 1934 to 1951, was from 1954 to 1961 the charismatic priest in charge of St Mary Aldermary in the City of London. The City is not the whole sprawling metropolis of Greater London, but the square mile in which London was founded by the Romans from 43 AD. It is London's chief financial district, and includes St Paul's Cathedral and the Tower of London as well as the church of St Mary Aldermary. There has been a church on this site for over 900 years; it was badly damaged but not destroyed by the Great Fire of 1666, and while the windows were shattered during the Blitz the building remained intact. It was patronised by a wealthy clientele – Barbara noted that 'There were a good many mink coats to be seen among its Sunday congregation' – and also by 'arty' people, among whom Canon Hood was said to be very comfortable.

The church is not very far from Fleet Street, so was within easy reach of Barbara's office in Fetter Lane.

In fact, Barbara heard the telephone in that church on 6 April 1955, and on 19 May she was there again on a cold and showery Ascension Day. 'I went to Freddy Hood's church at 1.15. The smell of incense from the solemnly sung Holy Communion at 12.15 still hung in the air …Afterwards Freddy Hood stood genially in his cassock talking to a rather excellent woman.' The telephone call and the speculation on its nature – a hostess asking one of the priests to luncheon or a cocktail party, perhaps – made an arresting starting point for *A Glass of Blessings*.

Unlike other novels on whose backgrounds I have previously written, there is curiously little material on *A Glass of Blessings* – scanty notes, no complete drafts, few reviews for the first edition in 1958, and not many fan letters either.

In the sub-section of the Pym Archive in the Bodleian entitled 'Papers relating to particular works' there is only one small notebook devoted to this novel. It is headed '*The Lime Tree Bower* (afterwards called *A Glass of Blessings*)'. 'This Lime-Tree Bower my Prison' is a poem by Samuel Taylor Coleridge; why Barbara chose this as the original title is unclear. 'A glass of blessings' is taken from the poem 'The Pulley' by George Herbert, the first stanza of which appears on the title page:

> When God at first made man,
>   Having a glasse of blessings standing by;
> Let us (said He) poure on him all we can:
>   Let the world's riches, which dispersed lie,
> Contract into a span.

Her notes are characteristically disjointed and rambling. One can imagine her pulling out her notebook to record some suitable item, possibly in a great hurry as she sat on a bus or in a cafe. She probably used many of these notes simply as aides-memoires, so didn't find it necessary to expand them, having no thought then that later others would be reading them. In this notebook she plunges straight in, without introduction, to a scene in a church.

One of the servers, a young man like Reg. [Reg was one of the Barnes neighbours in whom Barbara and Hilary took some interest. He eventually becomes Bill Coleman, owner of the Hillman Husky.]

Trinity Sunday – the Athanasian Creed sung in procession – the difficulty of writing a hymn about the Trinity – poor Father Faber's attempts – see 161 (?) in English Hymnal.

The Athanasian Creed is the third ancient Christian creed, from about the 6th century, and is very rarely used in modern worship because of its length and harshly didactic tone. The hymn in question, by Frederic William Faber (1814-1863, an Anglican who went over to Rome with Newman), begins rather inauspiciously, 'Have mercy on us, God most high, Who lift our hearts to Thee; Have mercy on us, worms of earth, Most holy Trinity.'

Barbara goes on:

It could be a lunch time Mass in a City church, a sparse congregation of office workers glad of the opportunity to fulfil their religious duties without too much inconvenience, and to hear, through the incense and the Sanctus bell, the shrill whine of the telephone.

Then she attempts a plot:

A fashionable church (which has lunch hour services) – a vicar and two curates living in a clergy house. All celibates. Then one gets married. His wife is 'unsuitable'.

One part is set on the Riviera where the vicar perhaps takes a party from his parish as he takes over the chaplaincy for some time. An elderly lady living there – in fact a ready-made 'flock [presumably English], and some unpleasantness between them and the one the vicar brings with him. Do we live in a villa or in a hotel?

Part I – In London. Part II – On the Riviera. Part III – Back again.

And she questions whether she should prefix these parts with quotations.

This idea of an exchange of vicars, and friction between the two congregations is, however, never developed. Next she considers some characters:

> The narrator – a widow or perhaps even divorced, rejected (or has this been overdone?) 39 years old, has lost her husband in the war and now grown used to her state – but quotes Donne…'these rags of heart'.

I searched high and low but could not find a quotation containing these words so I wonder if it was a slip of the pen, and she meant 'these rags of *time*,' which is a line from Donne's poem *The Sunne Rising*: 'Love all alike, no season knows, nor clime / Nor hours, days, months, which are the rags of time.' Barbara continues:

> She works for a firm of publishers and printers of learned books. Scholarly proofreading. Three of them in the department, 2 women, one man. Miss Enright who has never married; I, who had married but had not borne children, and Piers Longridge, 'brilliant' because he had a degree. He was a 'lapsed Catholic', Miss Enright a devout and practising one. RCs, I have found, are always described as 'lapsed' or 'very devout.' Perhaps the narrator falls in love with Piers.

Many of these notes of Barbara's are so odd and disjointed that it would not be useful to list them all. It might be better to tell you how from these notes we see some of the characters developing.

Fr Thames (at one time Fr Neptune was an alternative name – I wonder if the watery connection has some significance?) may have been suggested by Canon Freddy Hood, though Fr Thames perhaps lacks some of the latter's extroversion. Robert Smith likens Fr Thames to 'the redoubtable Fr Twisady', the real-life vicar of All Saints Church, Notting Hill, which also has, Robert says 'a somewhat evocative clergy-house.'

The new curate was at first to marry an 'unsuitable' wife, 'quite negligible, with a pretty face', who leaves him for somebody else. Later Barbara thought he should be 'rather tiresome and unstable – wanting to go over to Rome, to marry, [or] to enter a religious community. He might be seen coming out of Westminster Cathedral [London's Roman Catholic Cathedral], or Burns & Oates [a long-established Roman Catholic publisher], with an R.C. priest. He might have to go over to Shepherd's Bush to see some wise old priest.'

Bob Smith was living in London about this time, and his local church was All Saints, Shepherd's Bush in West London. I think that he had certain doubts, perhaps over the 'South India question', and possibly went to talk these over with 'some wise old priest', i.e. Fr Twisady, because Robert Liddell said in one of his letters, 'How is poor Robert, still carrying the cross? Or is he going back to Rome because of South India?'

[The Church of South India came into being when India gained independence in 1947, a union of Anglican and several Protestant churches. Because the Protestant churches were not governed by bishops ordained in apostolic succession, some traditionalist Anglicans refused to accept the validity of their ordinations and felt that 'the South India question' compromised the catholicity of the Church of England – this was as hotly debated in the 1950s as the issue of women bishops is today. Hazel Holt says that Bob Smith and Barbara 'fell out over this'.]

After a wobbly start as a widow or divorcée working as a proofreader with Piers and Miss Enright (later Miss Limpsett), Wilmet soon emerges as the Anglo-Catholic wife, with a 'solid broad-church' husband, an agnostic mother-in-law, and a comfortable and idle life style.

Piers was a proofreader from the start. The sight of him from the top of a bus entering a wine bar is based on an event noted by Barbara in April 1955. 'From a bus in The Strand I see Christopher Marsden of Oxford days – old Farquarson's Pliny lectures – he goes into Yates's Wine Lodge. Then I seem to remember hearing that he had not done well, been a disappointment, perhaps even taken to drink...' Piers to a T! But there is no speculation on Piers's sexual orientation.

Wilfred Bason was first conceived as Edward Herbert Gossage, a male cook-housekeeper 'of gentle birth,' but Barbara crossed out this name, and evidently ditched the 'gentle birth' as well. But the idea of him as a petty thief occurred to her quite early. 'Father Thames has something stolen by the male housekeeper. So petty, this kind of larceny – a little Fabergé trifle.' When Barbara was holidaying in Cornwall in August 1956, she wrote of 'the grey-bearded man waiting in the Antiques tea room at St Ives. A job for Mr Bason?' she asks herself.

Some characters are changed little from their first introduction, like Keith who in these notes is described as 'a friend of Piers who shares his flat – crew cut and windcheater. He is a model.' And Mary Beamish, 'a splendid little woman on committees, blood donor, church warden. Perhaps with an elderly mother who dies, then she is liberated.'

It was often the case that actual incidents in Barbara's life became embedded in her plots. One in this novel was the giving of blood. Her blood group was Rhesus Negative – 'that precious blood' as Miss Daunt proclaimed loudly, and, as we learn from Barbara's diaries, she gave it regularly – every 3 to 4 months from 1955-58 at least. On 4 May 1955 she writes, 'I give blood at the crypt of St Martin-in-the-Fields...I can imagine (for a novel) a little frail laden woman saying "Oh, I have given blood" and putting the others to shame.'

Another was the Portuguese lessons. On 19 August 1954 Barbara left on the SS *Alcantara* from Southampton, presumably disembarking at Lisbon. She does not mention having any companion with her, but I have learned since from Frances Atkin that she accompanied Barbara to Portugal, and they spent some weeks travelling around the country. On 7 October 1955, more than a year later, she writes 'First Portuguese class at Kings' College.' She may have been learning the language merely as a tourist, but she may also have thought it would be useful in her work – for there would have been articles in the journal *Africa* from the Portuguese colonies, Angola and Mozambique particularly. She continued going to classes regularly up to at least March 1958.

Miss Prideaux's mauve cardigan that Wilmet had sent to a jumble sale can be compared with the following notebook entry. 'At the Women's University Settlement I see Miss Casson wearing a dress that I sent to the jumble sale some time ago – and very nice it looks.' Barbara's experience in this Settlement was also used in the novel.

After many changes of name, the main characters of the novel are established, and there are extensive notes on Wilmet's visit to Rowena and Harry. The notebook ends with Father Ransome going to lodge with the Beamishes. There are no notes about later developments in the book. Barbara must surely have written more notes, or several drafts, but they have not survived. Because of the difficulty she had with the later novels, which she kept revising in the hope of attracting a publisher, many drafts and versions remain, but we know that Barbara felt justifiably confident that this novel would be accepted, so perhaps she felt it not necessary to keep her drafts. By 1957 she had already begun gathering material for *No Fond Return of Love*.

On 15 May 1957, Barbara wrote to Daniel George at Cape,

> I am hoping to post today or tomorrow the MS of the novel I have just finished, called *A Glass of Blessings*. I don't know whether to say much about it – it is probably better to leave you to read it first, but I may as well warn you that the heroine is not very nice and that the whole book is rather (too?) churchy. I have now reached the stage when it is impossible to look at it with any detachment.

Robert Liddell, with whom Barbara kept up a regular correspondence, wrote from Greece on Ascension Day 1957,

> I am delighted that *A Glass of Blessings* (a charming title) has been sent to dear Mr Cape but I had already (in one of his rare but sweet letters) heard that he had received it. He didn't actually say that he had read it, but he said that he would certainly offer to publish it. He expressed his pleasure in Miss Pym's work.

Jonathan Cape himself wrote to her two weeks later:

> I have enjoyed *A Glass of Blessings* and would like to publish it...*Jane & Prudence* didn't do so well as *Excellent Women*, but *Less Than Angels* sold pretty well. I think you have a secure public now, and I hope we will do well with *A Glass of Blessings*. So much depends upon the public, who are rather fickle these days...

The publishers were very fearful that any of Barbara's characters could be thought to be based on real people, and asked her to be very careful about this, as they feared a libel action. She did check Crockfords and other sources very carefully to see that she hadn't inadvertently used any real names. She replied, 'I haven't forgotten the worry of *Jane & Prudence* and my unfortunate reference to Marks and Spencers, so completely innocent on my part.'

Barbara had hoped that the book would appear in November, in time for Christmas sales, and indeed it was entered on the publishers' Autumn List. Robert Liddell was disappointed too. He wrote on 30 November, 'I regret waiting so long for *A Glass of Blessings*, which would be a comfort in the winter.'

However, Cape told her that a manuscript submitted after 1 May was usually too late for Christmas, and that their sales people found it difficult to sell fiction 'during the lean early months of the year before stocktaking', so publication was delayed until April 1958.

The delay between the announcement of the book in Autumn 1957 and its publication in April 1958 may have contributed to the lessening of its impact. Michael Howard wrote to Barbara, 'I'm sorry its press has not been more spectacular, but perhaps we can boost the sales along a bit during the [1958] autumn and Christmas season.'

A Glass of Blessings appeared on 14 April. Barbara wrote in her notebook, 'Only three reviews up to 29 April, none wholly good. [They say] my humour deserts me when dealing with romance, that I am tone-deaf to dialogue, that I am *moderately* amusing. [Are these] reviewers all women? Young women?'

Yes, they were all women, whatever their age. First out on 23 April was Brigid Brophy, writing in the now defunct *News Chronicle*.

> *A Glass of Blessings* is a curio: an eccentric light novel. It is told in the first person feminine by Wilmet, pretty, bored, rich and preoccupied with Anglo-Catholicism. With none of the religious person's intense fantasy-life, Wilmet simply has a foible for 'Fathers' and incense.

Husband and two potential flirtations interest her less than the Clergy House, a nest of celibacy. The story which results is milder than Trollope, and all the characters disintegrate when they speak, because their author is tone-deaf to dialogue; yet she describes them acutely, and her view is no less original than odd.

Next, Jocasta Innes in the *Evening Standard* on 27 April:

What happens when an attractive sophisticated woman finds after ten years of marriage that her husband is a bore? Wilmet Forsyth takes up church activities on the one hand and her best friend's dissolute brother on the other. Unfortunately the hu-mour which Miss Pym brings to the minutiae of parochial life deserts her when dealing with romance.

And lastly Patricia Hodgart in the *Manchester Guardian* on 29 April:

An Anglo-Catholic frolic garnished with a froth of Kensington conversation and a flutter of Fathers, *A Glass of Blessings* is catty, feminine and moderately amusing.

The *Daily Telegraph's* Peter Green liked it, and was the only one to note the homosexual element.

I don't normally raise much enthusiasm for spry little domestic novels sprayed with the incense of upper-middle-class Anglo-Catholicism, and with male characters called Piers or Rodney. But Barbara Pym's *A Glass of Blessings* caught me up short: her naive heroine, all unawares, falls in love with an obvious homo-sexual (though this is never explicitly stated) and the queer goings-on of male housekeepers and so on are described with catty accuracy.

There were longer reviews in *The Bookman*, April 1958, where Richard Church wrote:

It is a relief to escape, occasionally, from the contemporary school of violent writing, which so often conceals hysteria and sentimentality. Readers who share this feeling will enjoy *A Glass of Blessings*.

And by Austin Lee in *Now and Then*, Spring 1958:

> *A Glass of Blessings* is the first book I have read by Barbara Pym.
> I once saw a favourable review of a book of hers in a Church
> weekly, and it put me off. I cannot help a feeling of mistrust
> when I see a favourable review in an ecclesiastical paper, possi-
> bly because the only book of mine ever reviewed by one of
> them was described as 'blasphemous and boring'. I took excep-
> tion to the 'boring'.
>
> I enjoyed *A Glass of Blessings*. Although set in present day Lon-
> don, it is remote from the too urgent problems of our time and
> the world of the Angry Young Men, but this is part of its
> charm. Nothing earth-shaking happens, but once you begin,
> with the telephone ringing in the vestry at the back of the
> church into which the narrator, Wilmet Forsyth, has popped
> for a lunch-hour service, you find it hard to put the book
> down.

On this occasion, however, the ecclesiastical paper, the *Church Times*,
was not impressed:

> Barbara Pym's new novel *A Glass of Blessings* is small beer. Her
> story ambles gently along, without offence but without excite-
> ment either. It is certainly not without merit as a mildly
> amusing social commentary, but the reader is likely to be dis-
> appointed by the author's failure to engage a really lively
> interest. This is the fault chiefly of the central character Wilmet
> Forsyth, a wealthy and dissatisfied young woman with a com-
> fortable home in the West End, bored with her plodding civil-
> servant husband, and inclined to the mildest of mild flirtations
> to amuse herself. She professes interest in a neighbouring An-
> glo-Catholic church, whose clergy flit unconvincingly across
> the novel's course.
>
> But the religious aspect of the story never succeeds in penetrat-
> ing beneath the surface of a slightly precious and unworthy
> ecclesiasticism. As a novel deliberately set in a minor key, *A
> Glass of Blessings* has its points. But the tinkle of teacups is no
> substitute for the ringing of tocsins.

A reviewer for the *Oswestry and Border Counties Advertizer*, writing about a one-time resident, was eager to give her a good write-up:

> *A Glass of Blessings* is, to my mind, the best she had written in her cool, crisp style with its little touches of gently sardonic humour. Behind the novel one pictures a novelist with the outlook of a Jane Austen, and I hope that Barbara Pym is appreciated by connoisseurs of good writing as much as she deserves...The clergy and the various church supporters and the family circle of the principal character are sketched with delicacy but clarity, and I heartily recommend this book for quiet relaxation to any lover of first-class writing.

Robert Liddell was sent a complimentary copy, and on 23 April he wrote,

> Thank you very much indeed for your delightful book, big with blessings. I read it at a long happy sitting and look forward to taking it frequently to bed. A charming book, and I think your best – allowing for my predilection for *Some Tame Gazelle*. Such high church!...Wilmet is a lovely name for a heroine and I adore Mr. Bason and all the arrangements at the Clergy House. And (do tell me) do Anglo-Catholics now conform to R.C. fasting rules? I suppose they must, as Fr. Thames has something after midnight mass, and must have to celebrate again...I would have liked to know more of Miss Dove and Mrs Pollard, but I daresay we shall one day. It is nice to hear of Prudence again, and of poor Catherine. How does poor Robert (dear Bob) like it?
>
> Keith is absolutely sweet, and would have been so nice and efficient as a thurifer – perhaps, in a future work, he will see the light, and replace Eddie from the garage – but no, St Thomas's Shepherd's Bush would be nearer for him. I like Sibyl and Arnold very much too...Thank you again – and I hope you have excellent reviews.

And some weeks later he wrote again:

> Dear Elizabeth [Taylor] enjoyed *A Glass of Blessings* and drained it eagerly...she liked little Keith, of course. I told Penelope Gilliatt [she wrote for *Vogue*] in April how good you were and I

hope she will remember. [She didn't – at least I could find no review by her.] Dear Olivia [Manning] was very angry with a reviewer who thought you had a deficient sense of humour – and how right she was.

Barbara received a few more letters from friends and fans, mostly women, but again, fewer than for other novels. It would appear that because this novel was not widely reviewed it escaped the notice of many of her readers.

The first letter she received, on 15 April, was from her friend Peggy Makins, better known, perhaps, as Evelyn Home, Agony Aunt for *Woman*.

> Thank you so very much for *A Glass of Blessings* which I have gulped down and enjoyed extravagantly. A friend here at the office...has been reading it...and we agreed that your work is exactly like drinking some cool-tasting, innocent-looking beverage, which turned out in the end to be tipsy-making. In fact, without punning, just like a Pimms No. 1...Why, by the way, was he Father Bode. Was he a relation of Belinda and Harriet?

> I don't know that I quite swallowed Wilmet...I think perhaps that I don't believe in her because she doesn't sound quite warm enough to have made any impression on Harry or Piers. She was inquisitive about both, but not really stirred, I felt. But to be puzzled by a character pleases me...

> It didn't seem to me that Anglicanism really played much part in the novel. Wilmet didn't seem to believe anything very much, although she loved the look of various ceremonies and was awfully curious about the lives of the clergy...

On 9 May, Janet Ashbee wrote

> Dear Madam, I am venturing to send you the crit of an old friend of mine, a great reader and severe critic, and to tell you how enormously I have enjoyed *A Glass of Blessings*...it is such a relief to find a novel witty and clever, and minus adultery...Anyway I am most grateful for your beautiful easy writing, so clear and yet subtle.

This is her friend's 'crit' which she sent:

I have been very amused by *A Glass of Blessings* and, what one must call the 'goings-on' of that group of beings with the church for its centre…I felt it had an unusual success in a novel in that Barbara Pym does not lay down a plot or plan. There are her people, living and moving and talking – but it is left to the reader to think out what is left unsaid and to imagine the feelings left undescribed. In the end one has said and felt and, as it were, constructed the story. It is not often that an author takes one so into partnership.

Molly Hargreaves had met Barbara once, and wrote:

…thank you for *A Glass of Blessings*…I am ashamed to admit that I swallowed your glassful at one gulp, and no-one had a crumb to eat until it was finished…A certain phrasing in both your work and Elizabeth Taylor's had reminded me of Ivy Compton-Burnett…

A Miss Joan Simpson, from Wimbledon wrote:

I have very much enjoyed your new novel *A Glass of Blessings*, especially the subtle ecclesiastical background. However, the remark which you ascribe to Mr. Coleman at the top of p. 55 is curiously out of character. There are always four Sundays in Advent (variation only occurs in the number after the Epiphany or Trinity)…Please forgive me if you have already been overwhelmed by letters on this blemish, and accept my congratulations on a delightful story.

Robert Liddell, in *A Mind at Ease*, also commented on the conversation, which Wilmet overheard, in a note at the end of his essay on *A Glass of Blessings*, which reads:

There is one passage which may puzzle readers. 'Wouldn't believe the trouble we had over them', Mr. Bason was saying. 'It's really simpler when you haven't got any,' said Mr. Coleman. 'There were only four Sundays in Advent last year, I remember, so it can be a bit of a problem when to use them.' *They* are the rose-coloured vestments worn at Mid-Advent and Mid-Lent, as a change from the violet of the season, to encourage the Faithful. There is really no problem…as the fixed days are Gaudete

Sunday, third in Advent, and Laetare Sunday, fourth in Lent.

Of course Miss Simpson was right, there are always four Sundays in Advent, and it's very hard to imagine that Barbara was not well aware of the fact.

On 29 September 1962, Barbara wrote to Wren Howard at Cape, 'In the royalty statement which I received today I see that *A Glass of Blessings* is not mentioned, nor was it on the last statement. Does that mean that it has gone out of print?'

And he replied confirming that this was the case. She was very disappointed that she had not been informed, and that there was not even a file copy remaining. But of course, by 1962, the management at Cape was greatly changed.

A Glass of Blessings was reprinted in 1977, after Barbara's return to favour. Two English critics remarked that Wilmet was not an 'excellent woman'.

In the *Times Literary Supplement*, 30 September 1977, in a review entitled 'Brave are the Lonely', Anne Duchêne wrote:

> Wilmet Forsyth is rich and married, as well as elegant and attractive; so that although Wilmet is subject to 'useless little longings' – the whirls and eddies in the silent mind, at which Miss Pym excels – one cannot help feeling that Wilmet does not wholly qualify as a Pym heroine: her life does not require her to be brave so much as merely lucid.

Elizabeth Harvey (Henry's sister) wrote in the *Birmingham Post* on 23 September 1977:

> *A Glass of Blessings* [has] its sidelong humour and familiarity with high Anglican church matters…Wilmet, rather frivolous and vain, is more worldly than most Pym characters.

It does seem that *A Glass of Blessings* did not receive the level of attention of other of Barbara's novels, and that some of the critics were a little half-hearted. But there was one friend who consistently praised it – Philip Larkin. His correspondence with her began early in 1961, so he made no comment on it when it was first published, though in some undated and unattributed piece I found he wrote:

> *A Glass of Blessings,* like all her books, is dryly whimsical, Anglican, sharply observed, with autumnal currents moving under the surface. Wilmet Forsyth is almost my favourite Pym heroine.

When he wrote to her in March 1961 about *No Fond Return of Love* he said:

> …it was nice to meet Wilmet and Keith again. There is something very special about these two: They are memorable not only in themselves, but in their relation, as if Wilmet's reward for her 'sins' is this ridiculous unwanted incubus, or do I mean familiar, endlessly chattering of lovely homes and boiling things in Tide. There is a dreadful kind of justice about it. One feels she will never get rid of him.

And a few days later, in a letter to Maeve Brennan, he expresses similar sentiments:

> Yes, a Glass of Bs is my favourite BP, and Wilmet my favourite BP heroine. I think it had the strongest story line too, the way everyone but her seems to find love of some kind – even Rodney – and all she gets (as punishment, one feels, for her assignations with Piers) is the extraordinary Keith, whom one guesses she will never get rid of.

Barbara sent him a specially bound copy of *A Glass of Blessings* – 'a bibliographical curiosity, if nothing else,' she told him, 'and it is the only such copy in existence.' He replied:

> How very kind of you to send me such a unique and valuable 'item', as we librarians call these things. Really, I am most grateful. In many ways, it is my favourite among your books, and it means a great deal to me to have a 'personal' copy.

Larkin's unqualified approval would certainly have compensated for any perceived lack of warmth from others.

An earlier version of this paper was presented at the 2010 North American Conference in Cambridge, Massachusetts.

10

A Thankless Task?

The Development of
No Fond Return of Love

1957 – 1962

People blame one for dwelling on trivialities,
but life is made up of them. And if we've had one
great sorrow or one great love, then who
shall blame us if we only want the trivial things?

10
'A Thankless Task'?

In the previous chapter on *A Glass of Blessings* I said that I was disappointed at the paucity of material available, and much the same is true of *No Fond Return of Love*. For both novels I found only incomplete drafts and sparse notes; there is much more material for the later novels. Because of the constant rejection of *An Unsuitable Attachment* and *The Sweet Dove Died*, and the crossover between *The Sweet Dove Died, A Few Green Leaves,* and the attempted novel *Spring*, there are more drafts, failed attempts and revisions of them to draw on.

Barbara's novels are usually based on the world she knew and her own experience within it. When she deviated from this course, as in *An Academic Question*, she was less successful, and that novel is one of the least popular.

Before I come to an examination of the documents relating to *No Fond Return of Love*, I should like to suggest that one can immediately identify two influences in the novel, both coming from Barbara's own life experience at the time, namely her vicarious interest in her neighbours, and her attendance at a literary summer school.

The notebooks I consulted for this paper are those which cover the years 1957-1959. Disappointingly, they contain only a few jottings about the characters and situations in the novel, with little further indication of how she thought them up. Much of these notebooks is taken up with a day-to-day-account of the doings of the people who live in a house nearby – there is much more about the neighbours than about the novel!

At this time, Barbara and Hilary were living in Barnes, a district of southwest London. The sitting room of their house was on the upper floor, giving them a very good view of the road, and therefore an excellent opportunity to watch the comings and goings of their neighbours. Ever since her Oxford days, Barbara had been in the habit of following, or putting herself in the way of (as with Henry in the Bodleian), any man she liked the look of. She now pursued this vicarious interest with help from Hilary, and encouragement from Hazel Holt and Bob Smith. The neighbours in whom the sisters now took an interest were two young men, one of whom remained more or less permanently in residence, while the other was replaced from time to time by another. In fact, she had already 'used' them in *A Glass of Blessings* – the elder, as Mr Coleman with the Hillman Husky, and the younger as Keith. For several months Barbara noted all their observed movements in these notebooks, and she and Hilary wove a fantasy around this mysterious pair. 'A lovely saga,' says Hazel Holt in *A Lot to Ask*,[1] 'which involved us in various investigations, not only to St Laurence's [Church in Queen's Park]...but also to...a cemetery [with] informative gravestones, and a private hotel in the West Country.' Obviously this last is where Barbara got the inspiration for the Eagle House Hotel, its proprietress, and the mystery of the Forbes family. All this prying and 'stalking' became a major theme in *No Fond Return of Love*.

In the previous chapter I showed how a recent experience – the incongruous sound of a telephone ringing in the vestry, audible throughout the church during a lunch-time service -- made such an impression on Barbara that she determined to make it a feature of *A Glass of Blessings* – and indeed it became the memorable opening of the first chapter. In the case of *No Fond Return of Love* too, while she might not have yet known how it was all to pan out, Barbara had no doubts about her opening chapter. 'It could begin with a Swanwick-like conference,' she says.

Soon after Barbara had mailed the typescript of *A Glass of Blessings* to her publisher on 16 May 1957, she attended the Swanwick Writers' Summer School at the Hayes Conference Centre, once a 19th century gentleman's residence, more usually referred to merely as Swanwick [pronounced 'Swonick'] after the village near Alfreton in Derbyshire where it is situated.

These annual Summer Schools had started in 1949. Barbara may have chosen this course because it included the writing of short stories and TV/radio dramas, which she had previously attempted without any great success. Perhaps she was thinking about trying these literary forms again, and was looking for guidance.

Her personal engagement diary noted briefly the talks and visits to surrounding beauty spots which were the chief events of the six-day conference. I was fortunate enough to obtain from the archivist at Swanwick not only confirmation that Barbara did actually attend, but also the complete programme, and some notes on the speakers. John Dickson Carr, a prolific American crime writer who lived for many years in England gave a talk 'The Novel – the specialist speaks'. Phyllis Bayley, the then editor of *Vanity Fair*, spoke on women's magazines, Victor Menzies on writing for TV, Leslie Halward on radio drama; and others. There were also social events, including gramophone recitals and dancing (black tie preferred!).

Some of the talks were in the evening, to give the participants a chance to go on afternoon visits to Haddon Hall, a manor house dating from the 12th century, and to the hugely impressive Chatsworth, home of the Duke and Duchess of Devonshire.

In her notebook for August 1957 to April 1958 Barbara wrote what I assume to be a factual account, as it is dated Sunday 18 August, during the Summer School:

> Undenominational service in the chapel with the green leaves of huge rhododendron bushes outside the windows so that we might be in an aquarium or under water in the greenish light. We sing 'All things bright and beautiful' and an Indian lady plays the harmonium. But wouldn't she be a heathen, someone might ask anxiously? A rather intense woman with reddish hair cut in a fringe and dress with gathered skirt is older than one thinks
>
> At the end of the long tables the woman (or women) who happen to be sitting there serve out the soup and the portions of food. (Men very seldom do.) Often an unmarried woman does it, perhaps it satisfies some deep need, something finer than

mere bossiness. At the end of the meal plates are piled up and taken to the tables by the hatch, but it will do if one goes away carrying just a small thing like a jug of custard.

One sits in a basket chair in the vinery where the grapes hang already ripe. It could be an orangery or old conservatory. Splendid place for long sad conversations.

Much of that went into Chapter 1.

In the same notebook Barbara introduces Dulcie, said to be the charac-ter most like Barbara herself, Viola, based on the 'intense woman' mentioned above, and Miss Foy, the woman serving the food.

There is only one draft of the novel. This is in three parts, two hard-backed and one thin soft cover exercise books. The first book is a draft of Chapters 1–6 and part of 7, hand-written on the rectos only, with notes, presumably added later, on the versos. Most of the notes are quite trivial, but about a third of the way through is an extensive annotation, showing that Barbara was still undecided about the character of her heroine, and how to depict her:

> What sort of a person is Dulcie? What has her life been? She had loved somebody who jilted her and never really loved again, perhaps taking refuge in the cosiness of other people's lives – even letting her appearance go a little. She did not want to be hurt yet she could look on the hurts of others with a kind of detachment that sometimes shocked her. He had been called Clive, he had been a worthless person, really no good. She had been going to bolster him up, the thing all women like to do, so that pleasure as well as love had been taken away. Is it in any way more poignant to have loved somebody unworthy?

There is little else of note in this book. The draft of the six plus chapters appears on casual reading to be very like the finished version. The other hard-backed notebook contains a draft of Chapters 12–23, which again seem very like the final version. There is no draft surviving for Chapters 9–11 and 24–25.

The thin exercise book, which includes a draft of the rest of Chapter 7 and Chapter 8, is rather more interesting as it also contains notes. These

he is, and he eventually fades out of the picture altogether.

Viola is desperate to get married – perhaps in the end she might get Dulcie's Clive [later to become Maurice Clive]. It would be better if Dulcie's uncle and aunt lived somewhere nearer to Aylwin, as well as to his brother's parish.

Viola, perhaps, hasn't known Aylwin Forbes well – but on seeing her in the gardens in her red canvas shoes he remembers her as 'that rather embarrassingly intense woman' who had wanted to talk about his work.

Perhaps the clergyman is Aylwin's cousin. His brother and mother run the hotel. Something disgraceful about the brother. 'An interesting family.'

In the next two notebooks covering April 1958 to October 1959, Barbara writes down some thoughts which she did in part incorporate in the completed novel:

Walking across a common to the house with literary associations where, to her surprise, a woman is holding a small Bring and Buy Sale.

One of Aylwin Forbes's relatives (?The one who keeps the Eagle House Private Hotel) is thought to be related distantly to the noble county family whose house is open to the public. There would be memorials in the church. Piers and Keith going round the house. Wilmet?

In the suburban garden Senhor MacBride-Pereira is reading Eça de Queiroz [a realist Portuguese writer of the second half of the 19th century] and eating sugared almonds (he likes the mauve ones best), when he sees... what? Some vital happening. Aylwin Forbes embracing Laurel in the garden.

Mrs Beltane waters her plants with a special little plastic watering can shaped like a swan, a curious lapse of taste one feels.

Aylwin Forbes's mother – rather stark and formidable old West Country woman rather living in the past. Enjoying discomfort. No fire in her bedroom. Wearing a tweed deerstalker and ankle-length old musquash coat. Walks in the moors. 'It looks bad.' How can the resident proprietress be supervising the 'cuisine' when she's doing this?

The tablecloths were always put on the tables in the Dining Room on Palm Sunday – ready for the Easter visitors. It was easier to have that kind of routine when you have a clergyman son – going with the church's year, as it were. Though these new plastic ones could really be left on all the year round. At the same time the big stuffed eagle in the hall – from which the hotel took its name Eagle House Private Hotel – was given its annual cleaning with one of the Hoover tools.

The Residents' lounge must also be refurbished, 'a corner of the Residents' lounge' picture on the brochure gave little idea of its true 'flavour'.

Eventually Barbara must have sorted out these thoughts until she arrived at a workable plot – exactly how we really can't tell. The novel, still entitled *A Thankless Task*, was completed and sent to the publisher in July 1960, but Daniel George, the Executive at Cape with whom Barbara usually dealt, wrote to her:

Dear Barbara,

Some of us here are not very happy about the title of your new novel. It is of the kind that is perceived to be exquisitely appropriate once the book has been read but until then, and from a selling point of view, is not very enticing.

Can you think of something different?

When Barbara came up with *No Fond Return of Love*, which she may have found in a poem in Sir Arthur Quiller-Couch's edition of the *Oxford Book of English Verse* (as I did), Daniel George replied

As I thought, the poem is by Fanny Greville – and you have misquoted it: the word should be KIND, not FOND,

I ask no *kind* return of love,
  No tempting charm to please;
Far from the heart those gifts remove,
  That sighs for peace and ease.

The syntax is odd. 'That' in line 4 must refer to the heart, not the gifts. But I think we shall stick to the title unless you come up with something more appealing.

Then Barbara thought she would prefer simply *No Return of Love*, but that too met with disapproval.

> Your preference for 'No Return of Love' as a title, without either the 'Kind' or the 'Fond', has, I am afraid, caused some dismay to our publicity and advertising people. They are very anxious that the 'Fond' be retained (despite that fact that the original verse has 'Kind') as they feel that 'No Return of Love' is too flat and is no better than the original 'Thankless Task.'

So, under this pressure, Barbara agreed to *No Fond Return of Love*. It was published in February 1961.

Robert Liddell wrote from Athens on 27 February,

> Dearest Barbara
>
> Thank you for your letter, and for the delightful novel – I loved the private hotel, and all the search. But I do not like your heroine carrying on with a divorced man. One sees, of course, that it comes of being not a good churchwoman…I like the Sedges very much too, and all the settings are admirably done. Of course there is never enough incense for me, but I daresay you are right to economise with it. I read it more or less at a sitting, on a grey Sunday, and am delighted to have another Pym to re-read. I was pleased to see Wilmet and Keith again, though for so brief a glimpse – I wished for a bit more of Miss Spicer.

This letter seems to me a little lukewarm. I don't think *No Fond Return of Love* was one of Liddell's favourites. In *A Mind at Ease*[2] he sums up the novel thus:

> There are perhaps too many subjective cameras clicking away; they produce a great richness of detail, but there is not a strong enough central interest to give it sufficient coherence.

After Bob Smith, now in Nigeria, had read the book, and declared his enjoyment of it, Barbara wrote to him:

> Dearest Bob
>
> I'm so glad the book arrived safely and that you have enjoyed it. You are one of the few who know how truly B. Pym it is –

but really Dulcie had an easy time of it compared with us searching for Bill's church, didn't she? I am not pleased myself with the book really, but have begun to think it a little better since people seem to have liked it so much and I have had some very good reviews – the TLS [*Times Literary Supplement*] most kind, and *Tatler* most rapturous! But I think *A Glass of Blessings* is better, though it was not nearly so well reviewed.

British Books, a monthly publication enjoying a sneak preview of books before publication, wrote in its January 1961 issue,

> Miss Pym's Austenish sense of wit and her sugar-coated satire are superbly displayed in this novel of a group of research workers and the complexities of their relationships – in particular of one, Dulcie Mainwaring, who discovers that in her neighbours in suburbia there is abounding grist for any researcher's mill. A brilliant, sparkling book.

John Davenport's was the first newspaper review, in the *Observer*, 5 February 1961:

> Miss Pym is a clever writer, but *No Fond Return of Love* tends rather to doodle along in a Jane Austenish manner without that great lady's method. The evocation of the north London suburb, of the west-country town – these are admirable. The feeling of Ovaltine, of deep apricot pie, of pink plastic apostle spoons, of little Anglican aptnesses and ineptitudes – all these are beautifully done here, but Dulcie Mainwaring somehow eludes one; and so does Aylwin Forbes, a mysterious figure in a mysterious world, the literary-academic.
>
> There is some good sharp spinsterish laughter, and laughter of any kind is a thing to be grateful for; but I found myself caught in a yawn. A reasonably civil, Sundayish one, I hope.

The *Evening Standard* on 7 February said:

> Suburban life under the microscope, with the minutiae sharply focused and detailed with affection: gentle, dowdy young woman, retired domestic help, handsome vicar etc. Unrevolutionary, but well done.

Hilary Seton of the *Sunday Times* wrote on 19 February:

> A social comedy of people on the edge of life, refined to emotional anaemia. Aridity, intellectual pretensions and loneliness as youthful hopes collapse – Miss Pym draws her group of characters with her customary acuteness, honesty and surface humour – talk about the smile on the face of the tiger!

Siriol Hugh-Jones's 'rapturous review', as Barbara termed it, was in *The Tatler* on 15 February 1961:

> *No Fond Return of Love*, by Barbara Pym, is a delicious book, refreshing as mint tea, funny and sad, bitchy and tender-hearted, about what it is like to be a fading lady in her early thirties living in North London and trying to soothe the niggling pangs of disappointed love with hot milky drinks and sensible thinking. Dulcie Mainwaring has a broken engagement, a large dowdy house, a teenage niece and a cross friend called Viola Dace who hopelessly loves the glamorous literary figure Aylwin Forbes. The background is suburban literary-fringe life, parish churches, weird seaside hotels, and the polite impingement of people who do not much like each other but share a common loneliness...
>
> I love and admire Miss Pym's pussycat wit and profoundly un-soppy kindliness, and we may leave the deeply peculiar, face-saving, gently tormented English middle classes safely in her hands.

The *Church Times*, which reviewed most, if not all of Barbara's novels, described it as 'Sensitivity without sentiment':

> Barbara Pym's novels are not everyone's cup of tea. She pitches her narrative in a deliberately minor key, and occupies herself chiefly with the cool, detached observation of undistinguished men and women, putting their motives and their foibles under the microscope of her exact inquisition.
>
> Her new novel *No Fond Return of Love* falls precisely into this category. It is a clever but sometimes rather tedious examination of the social behaviour of a likeable spinster who fears that a broken engagement has put her on the shelf for good, and of

a conceited, intellectual snob who edits a literary journal. His marriage is on the rocks, and Dulcie Mainwaring, by a persistent curiosity about him and his affairs, ends up by so involving herself in his life that her strictly academic interest turns into something like love.

Students of the niceties of middle-class social quirks and mannerisms will derive quiet pleasure from Miss Pym's delicate and almost feline appreciation of her chosen metier. She has a sense of humour and fun, never too obvious, which compensates for the dreariness and futility of most of her characters. And her writing has style, something rare enough in contemporary novels to make the reader truly thankful for at least one small mercy.

The *Daily Telegraph* on 24 February 1961:

Dulcie Mainwaring, thirtyish, unsophisticated, unmarried and middle-class, devotes her considerable leisure to prying into the reasons which caused the marriage of a handsome male acquaintance to go on the rocks. Characters and situation acutely, but not too cynically, handled.

The *Glasgow Herald*, however, was scathing:

No Fond Return of Love by Barbara Pym is unusual in being set in the vague dusty world of libraries, catalogues, and research. A silly love story – or stories – is much bedevilled with trivia, and perhaps ought to have been published for the deck chair season, when the fact of there not being enough cauliflower au gratin for two might achieve importance.

Many fans were inspired to write to Barbara. Some of these were her friends, or destined to become friends, but others were total strangers. Rachel Cecil, the wife of Lord David Cecil, wrote from Cranborne, Dorset, on 31 October 1961. Her husband later became one of Barbara's champions.

Dear Miss Pym

I have just finished reading *No Fond Return of Love*, and feel I must tell you what enormous pleasure it gave. It was sheer en-

joyment from the delightful beginning – whetting one's appe-
tite at the Conference – to the surprising and satisfying end
with Senhor MacBride Pereira sucking his mauve sugared al-
mond.

The characters are all so well drawn, and so amusing. I love
Mrs Forbes – Aylwin – Miss Lord – Father Benger – one is
kept amused all the way through – and with such subtle comedy – yet one does take Dulcie seriously and her inner
comments on life. It is so well written too.

I can imagine the suburb so well, and the gardens, and Tavis-
combe. The whole novel builds up so well – that it becomes a
real picture of life – and one really cares about what happens to
Dulcie. Although most of it is splendid comedy, I like the little
gleams of thoughtfulness, and even sadness. I must thank you
for giving us so much enjoyment. I haven't enjoyed a present-
day novel so much for years.

Barbara's old friend Honor Wyatt, wrote:

Dearest Barbara

Delicious! First I read it, then Prue [her daughter] read it and
we have so much enjoyed saying 'Isn't it lovely where…' to each
other…I thoroughly enjoyed the conference – it reminds me so
much of gathering at a place near Devizes where I lecture sometimes. You ought to go on a course at Denman College some
time, the Women's Institute's 'Countrywoman's College'. All
ladies thrilling to male lecturers, you'd find it an absolute
feast…

Peggy Makins was better known as Evelyn Home, the agony aunt on
the weekly magazine *Woman*. Barbara had corresponded with her for
years, and Peggy had done her best to try to get Barbara's short stories
published.

Dear Barbara,

Now I am very nearly through *No Fond Return of Love* for the
2nd time, I am beginning to believe that it may prove one of
my favourites, as *Jane & Prudence* is becoming also. Not yet being again at the end, I recall it as rather a surprise – I just didn't

expect Dulcie to want such close acquaintance with Aylwin really. I very much enjoyed the conference at the beginning, especially because I've been to Swanwick and remember the incredible lack of air in the big lounge.

You didn't mention the curious oneness of the taste of the food there. I remember thinking that the sponge cake at tea tasted precisely the same as the sliced mutton at lunch, except for the texture and temperature of the two foods...

And from Isobel Anslow, Richmond, Surrey, on 1 April 1962:

Dear Barbara,

I bought a copy of *No Fond Return of Love* about a couple of months ago. I want you to know how much I have enjoyed reading it. All the little incidences you relate, e.g. the arrival at the Eagle House Hotel; the meal on the train; the Vicar's invitation for Dulcie to live in Miss Spicer's flat and all its implications. Dulcie Mainwaring's reactions to her circumstances remind me so much of myself. Next to *Excellent Women* I like it best...

Readers unknown to Barbara were also eager to express their delight at her latest novel. This is from a reader in Hampstead:

I write, feeling a little silly for so doing, to say how much I have enjoyed your book *No Fond Return of Love*. I am in the middle of a spell of feeling particularly overworked and under-appreciated and didn't feel to have a laugh left in me, when, on Saturday night I started to read your book in bed!

Sunday was cluttered with visitors all day and I kept longing to sneak away and revive myself with another chapter. In bed once more I snatched it up with the intention of finishing it before going to sleep – but then I thought I must spin the pleasure out a bit. So, I finished it this morning before embarking on wash day and all the time it has made me laugh out loud. Thank you for lifting me out of my mild depression and drawing my attention once more to the endless fun of life.

I have been your devoted reader ever since *Some Tame Gazelle*. I am 50 and have a married daughter, a Hungarian son-in-law, an alarming 'sixth-former' daughter and an Inspector of Taxes for a husband – all delightful, but I love to escape from time to time into your world, so don't ever stop writing – there must be thousands of others who feel the same.

A Margaret Hillsden from Surrey wrote more succinctly:

What a joy it was to read your latest book *No Fond Return of Love*. All the characters appear real. True to life, with the combined interest of London. Many thanks for producing such an excellent book.

And from Hornsby, New South Wales, Lucy wrote:

I have just finished your book *No Fond Return of Love* and I want to tell you how much I enjoyed it. The faint ridiculousness, the wistfulness of London suburbs in Autumn, the clear visual pictures of it all, have pleased me very much.

This next rather curious letter is not an appreciation of the book, which the writer hasn't yet read, but rather a personal, and despite the writer's own estimation, somewhat trite comment:

Dear Madam

As an ordinary reader I hope to read your novel *No Fond Return of Love* recently published.

May I please take the liberty of making a comment on the subject of marriage, which novelists sometimes write about? That is to say that some of the most satisfactory I know of were contracted when both the partners were middle-aged or even elderly. (I know of three such cases just in my own vicinity.) I think that this fact is interesting and, perhaps, shows the value of age and experience in these matters. (Not, of course, that I am implying that people should deliberately wait until they are middle-aged to marry as a matter of policy.) With apologies for writing you…

Finally a male fan, a naval Commander from Cirencester:

I must write to thank you for the pleasure you have given me in reading *No Fond Return of Love* – the delightful way in which you have drawn the various characters…if you are in London between July 1-7 come and have a drink at the Travellers Club with yours gratefully, Francis Cadogan.

[*Burke's Peerage* tells us that in 1962 Commander Francis Charles Cadogan, RN(Ret), FRGS, FZS, grandson of the 4th Earl Cadogan and a veteran of the Boer War and both world wars, was 77 years old and had been married for 48 years, so the invitation to meet him in London for a drink at his club was perfectly proper!]

No Fond Return of Love appears to be the novel which has most often been dramatised, and, I believe, the only one performed live before a public audience. Firstly in October 1965 it was dramatised for BBC Radio by Elizabeth Proud, who also played Mrs Williton and Miss Lord. [Elizabeth Proud was a founding member of the Barbara Pym Society, and served as its first Chairman.]

The programme of the Barbara Pym Literary Weekend at St Hilda's College, Oxford, in August 1993 included scenes from *No Fond Return of Love* adapted by Georgia Powell, granddaughter of the famous writer Anthony Powell, and directed by Georgia's father Tristram, a radio producer/director. All the parts were played by four actors, three of whom were professional, who had all recently worked with Tristram Powell.

In 1988 the Vicar of All Saints' Church in Whetstone, North London, prepared and directed an adaptation of *No Fond Return of Love* which had three performances at the All Saints' Arts Centre. In 1994 it was presented at The Man in the Moon Theatre in Chelsea, where it ran for three weeks, and, according to Hazel Bell, it was also done in Australia in 1994. A more elaborately staged version was performed back at the All Saints' Arts Centre in November 1997. Hazel Bell, long-time member of the Barbara Pym Society and a former editor of *Green Leaves*, went to see it, and wrote about it in March 1998:

> I attended the performance of *No Fond Return of Love* on 29th November 1997 in Whetstone, and found a truly Pymian occasion. A wet night: we arrived in the church hall to find a small audience including two nuns, their habits glistening with raindrops. Chocolate biscuits and various, mostly soft, drinks were being sold at a table – no, not sold, but giving opportunity for

donations, because of the parish licensing system. We felt the appropriate Pymian spirit pervading not only the stage, but the entire hall.[3]

No Fond Return of Love was the last novel for which Barbara did not have a fear of rejection. After this, her writing career took a downturn, and it was many years before it rose again. It was therefore, all the more gratifying to read in Ian Jack's column in *The Guardian* on 1 January 2011:

> On Boxing Day I finished Barbara Pym's *No Fond Return of Love*, as greedily as I used to polish off my gift box of Liquorice Allsorts. I shouldn't have been reading it at all – I bought it for my daughter – but there is no stopping with a Pym novel after the first accidentally read page. After this book appeared in 1961 her publishers decided they wanted no more. What fools they were.

An earlier version of this paper was presented at the 2011 North American Conference in Cambridge, Massachusetts.

11

A Publication History of The Sweet Dove Died

1963 – 1970

Leonora liked to think of her life as calm of mind,
all passion spent, or, more rarely, as emotion
recollected in tranquility. But had there ever really
been passion, or even emotion?

11

A Publication History of The Sweet Dove Died

After the shock and disappointment of the rejection by Cape in 1963 of *An Unsuitable Attachment*, and further rejection by many other publishers, Barbara Pym put this novel aside and started on a new one. The first mention of this is in her notebook for 1963. On 16 October she wrote, 'I have started to write another novel, as I knew I would eventually, but I don't get on very fast.' It was not until December 1964 that she wrote rather sadly to Philip Larkin, 'I have written seven or eight chapters of a new novel. Of course in the end it will turn out not to be any good, perhaps, but I may as well write something even if only for private circulation among a few friends...' In *A Lot to Ask*, Hazel Holt says that the inspiration for the new novel was, in part, Richard Roberts, who had been introduced to her and Hilary by Bob Smith in the summer of 1962, and with whom she embarked on a hopeless romantic relationship. At its inevitable end, she made use of the experience when she started writing again.

Richard, called Skipper by his close friends, has, of course, no exact counterpart in *The Sweet Dove Died*. He had no obvious personality traits in common with Humphrey, though his interest in antiques and ownership of an antique shop translated to the novel. He was too old (in his 30s) to be James, though his behaviour sometimes belied his age, and the idea of 'anything coming' from such a relationship applies equally to James and Leonora in the novel and to Richard and Barbara in real life. There is an element of Ned in him too, as when Barbara describes 'his very spoilt little Bahamian mood, full of euphoria, money and sex talk'.

In her 1962 notebook, even before she met Richard, she had jotted down a few items which later appear in some form in the book. She writes 'a little Italian bowl really pleases me, though it is chipped, and I begin to wonder if I'm getting to the stage when objects could please more than people or (specifically) men.' And after meeting Richard, the following idea occurs to her. 'A man, dealer in antiques, goes to a parish jumble sale in search of Victoriana and there gets involved in things he would rather not have experienced.' In 1963 she notes, 'The middle-aged woman with an Italian lover' who enjoys Guinness, 'A wet day in Hampstead – Keats's House – the engagement ring he gave Fanny B.', and 'walking in Bond Street I see a young man sitting alone in a grand antique shop, presumably waiting for customers. A woman admirer might be a great nuisance always coming to see him.'

On 26 September 1965, when her relationship with Skipper was waning, she writes 'After the dentist, the Wimpole Street Buttery. A delicious creamy cake tasting of walnuts. Now Skipperless, one begins to understand "compensatory eating".'

The furniture repository episode in *The Sweet Dove Died* was occasioned by a similar event in Barbara's life, when Bob Smith, who was returning to Nigeria, offered to lend furniture to Barbara, and also to another friend – though in this case there was probably no dispute, but possibly a misunderstanding. All these ideas and little incidents found their way into *The Sweet Dove Died*.

There are in the Bodleian Library several drafts of the novel, the earlier ones, all undated, telling a very different story from the version eventually published. One, the earliest I think, appears to be the beginning of a novel called *Spring*, an unusually succinct title for Barbara. Chapter One begins startlingly with Violet Couchman saying 'No, Lionel, a fox's droppings are *grey* and pointed at both ends.' Lionel is Violet's first husband; the two of them, together with her second husband Hilary Couchman, are visiting Phoebe, a newcomer to their village. Lionel lives in a hut at the bottom of the Couchmans' garden, where he is more or less independent, though hot dinners are sent down from the house. Hilary, the second husband, wouldn't mind him living in, but Lionel says 'It might cause a scandal in the village if I lived in the house – few of these good people are familiar with what one might call polyandry.' And in any case, he is a sociological researcher and 'likes to keep all his data with him'.

Before they arrived, Phoebe had been sitting in the little front room of her cottage where Anthea Wedge, whose literary remains Phoebe was to work on, had written her poems and the journal Phoebe was preparing for publication. 'Phoebe remembered that James had promised to visit her, but that had been after dinner when they had both had a lot to drink. He said he would like to see her again, but he hadn't even kissed her goodnight.'

When her visitors left, 'Phoebe flopped down in an armchair. Her first experience of village social life had been exhausting…she wondered when James would get in touch with her.' Later she has a meal with her friend Rose Culver, who, according to Violet, 'does good works' in the village, but had once had a love affair with a married man who worked in Africa but came home each summer.

Two further undated manuscripts are cited as 'Typescript draft and incomplete carbon copy of *The Sweet Dove Died*'. In fact, both copies are incomplete, each lacking whole chapters and individual pages. However, the carbon copy includes Chapter 2, and a few other pages which the original lacks – so the two need to be used together. They seem to be an expanded version of *Spring*. The characters mentioned above are retained, and are joined by an alcoholic 'resting' actor, a vicar previously involved in a sex scandal, a cleaning lady and her electrician son who is over-familiar with his customers, an ex-Anglican priest turned married RC layman and novelist, and several others all living in an unnamed village.

This draft opens like the published version, with Leonora having been picked up by Humphrey and James at the sale room, but apart from some dallying in the country between James and Phoebe, and some socialising with the villagers, little more is heard of them. Ned makes a benign appearance towards the end, with Rose and Leonora encouraging him to take over Phoebe's cottage in the country. It ends with Leonora hoping that a relationship might develop between Rose and Ned, while she continues her liaison with James. All very bland, I thought, a rambling plot with far too many characters and subplots, and no real focus. The acerbity and deep feeling of the final work is completely absent.

Nevertheless, this must have been the version, tidied up and improved no doubt, though I found no evidence for this, that she sent to Wren Howard at Jonathan Cape on 5 June 1968, saying:

> I hope, you will feel that this may well be a good time to pub-lish another novel of mine, in view of the library reprints of *Some Tame Gazelle* and *Excellent Women*, the Woman's Hour adaptation of *No Fond Return* not so long ago, and the occa-sional enquiries you and I have had about when another novel might be expected. I was also encouraged by a talk with Kath-leen Shannon some months ago to feel that I should at least have one more try and let you have the first refusal of this book. I think you will find *The Sweet Dove Died* sharper and faster moving than the book I sent you in 1963…

Howard's son Michael replied:

> I know that my Father has in the past always corresponded with you about your books, but as you know, when you sent in the manuscript of *The Sweet Dove Died* he was away in poor health, and I am sorry to say that he is not yet strong enough to return to the office.
>
> It, therefore, falls to me to write sadly to convey to you the consensus of opinion about your new novel, which is, I am afraid, that we do not feel it likely to sit happily in the kind of list which we have now, or to make a mark strong enough to justify its presence there in your eyes or in ours. You mentioned that you thought we would find it sharper and faster-moving than *An Unsuitable Attachment*; but that doesn't really seem to be the case: the neatness and irony which were so much a char-acteristic of your earlier books has rather softened, and while such good nature is most lovable in an author, readers unfortu-nately seem to relish greater asperity in their books!

The fact that he speaks of irony softening, and 'such good nature' proves, I think, that Barbara sent him a version primarily about the Village community, because 'soft' and 'good nature' are words hardly applicable to *The Sweet Dove Died* as we know it.

Next she sent it to Longmans Green, who rejected it on similar grounds, and then to Chatto and Windus. They kept it for six weeks or more, but finally rejected it.

In September 1968 Barbara sent the novel to Philip Larkin for his opinion, and, as she said to Robert Smith

> ...he told me what was really wrong with it – too many characters, and the action really should concentrate more on Leonora, the real centre of the book. I have to fill out her character and write more bits of horrible Ned. So I haven't sent it anywhere else, but have been thinking how I might rework it.

Barbara must have spent most of 1969 rewriting the novel along the lines suggested by Larkin. Phoebe and Rose Culver were retained, with less important roles, but all the other characters were eliminated. Some of them, I am fairly sure, were adapted for use later in *A Few Green Leaves*. Certainly the fox's droppings found their way there!

The revised version went to Macmillan in January 1970. James Wright wrote,

> I read *The Sweet Dove Died* with real interest. It seems to me beautifully done, with quiet wit and sensitive awareness of how preposterous people are. I enjoyed it greatly, smiling at its humour and felicity of style and the perfection of its taste, but alas it seems to me a chancy commercial proposition. On commercial grounds alone, I am afraid we shall very reluctantly have to say no. I am genuinely sorry about this but in returning the manuscript to you I would like to thank you for allowing us to read your charming book, and I do hope that somebody else will have the courage to publish it.

She then sent it to Peter Davies Ltd, whose Mark Barty King sent a long letter of refusal on 29 October 1970:

> I know you will be very disappointed, but I must return to you your novel *The Sweet Dove*...We had a number of reports on the book, some contradictory, and I think it would be con-

structive if I repeated some of the readers' comments:

'This is a novel of quiet melancholy and understatement; the subject is socially limited (as in Ivy Compton-Burnett) but the author is in full control and allows herself no self-indulgence. She writes with continued fluency and precision and the reader's interest is maintained without the need for high-pitched emotion or violent dramatics.'

'A synopsis of the plot of this novel does not do it justice, though it may indicate the fineness of construction which eliminates superfluous elements. Its strength lies in the precision of the characterisation, the well-wrought dialogue, the attention to detail that makes it something out of the ordinary. The portrait of Leonora is superb and beside it the other characters may seem faintly delineated, especially, perhaps, Phoebe Sharpe, who is always seen indirectly. But this single-mindedness gives the book additional strength.'

'This is a slight, almost trivial story, depending almost entirely on accurate characterisation. It is meant to be casually witty, relying on the small episodes of life, and the way people tend to be selfish however noble their motives. To some extent it succeeds in this although one grows a little tired of the incessant effort. It is all very ingrown and a little decadent, although not in a really interesting way. One feels that the constant play on minutiae becomes rather claustrophobic. No particular point is brought out; the book drifts off to nothing in the end and as it had never had real substance one feels that all it is remarkable for is the close and exact observation of human trivialities.'

'My impression is that the writer has basically nothing to say but has a facile and clever-clever sense of the ridiculous which she has here tried to extend into a novel. But there is a wearisomeness about it and the wit is never pungent enough to bring the pages alive. The whole book left me feeling vaguely uneasy, a slight feeling that I would rather not have read it. I think the author has talent but not enough for a full-length novel unless she can support her rather flimsy characters with a stronger plot.'

'This author can write well and I found the feline analysis of

Leonora, James, Hubert [sic] and Phoebe vastly entertaining and shrewd but in a circumstantial way. Indeed beyond the half way mark of the book I discovered that the theme lost interest and the manner of writing, for all its devastating accuracy, turned slightly sour.'

My own feeling [continues King] is that *The Sweet Dove* is a most unusual novel which doesn't quite come off. There is much that is praiseworthy in the book: your tight control, grasp of detail, observation of human foibles, petty jealousies etc. The characters, though fey and insecure are quite recognisable as types – rather self-consciously dedicated to gentility, appreciation of beauty, the cultivated arts – and unmistakably bitchy with it. I would place it as being not far off a minor tour de force, because its close focus and small-angle lens point up very effectively the lives and interests of its characters...

A touch more styled elegance, a slightly sharper humour, a more surprising plot...the whole thing might have been carried off. Yet, paradoxically, it is your refusal to overstate that is in some ways the most impressive element about the book.

In the final analysis, I have to conclude that the book is simply not inventive enough to hold the reader's attention all the way through. I hope I have made it clear, however, how accomplished we feel the book is. I should be most interested to see anything else you may have written, or write in the future.

Barbara thanked him and the other readers' for 'the interesting and encouraging comments provided,' and told him of her earlier published work, which she had neglected to mention before as 'a book must be judged on its own merits.'

King replied that taste in fiction had changed greatly over the past 20 years, and that *The Sweet Dove Died* would, he thought, have been acceptable in 1950, or even 1960, but in 1970 public taste demanded books with a 'strong narrative drive'.

The senior editor at Hodder's reported,

The *Sweet Dove Died* is beautifully done, delicate, quietly witty, with a nice amused awareness of how preposterous these people are – both the actual characters who are real and capable of emotions, however complacent, unrealistic or selfish, and the peripheral characters of lonely, slightly desperate women and their ambiguously sexed young men. But this piece of fiction is deliberately elegant and tiny, about elegant and tiny emotions, and anything so quiet is commercially unviable these days, except perhaps in a very small edition. Personally I enjoyed reading it, both for its skill of writing and because it is in perfect taste.

Then to Macdonald & Co., to Collins (signing herself Tom Crampton); to Secker & Warburg under the heading "Leonora, by Tom Crampton", who, in complete contrast to King's helpful analysis, merely acknowledged receipt and asked for 4s postage 'for its return in the event of rejection.' To Weidenfeld & Nicolson, to John Murray, who also required the postage to be paid if the MS was returned, but who rejected it more civilly with,

> We have given *The Sweet Dove Died* a most sympathetic reading and now have our readers' reports on this book. One of our readers especially is an admirer of your other books and I have enjoyed the two that I have read. I am sorry to tell you that in our opinion *The Sweet Dove* seems to us a far weaker novel than the others and not one that we feel we could sell successfully...
>
> Although we appreciate the keen perception of your characterisation, in the opinion of our readers the plot of this book is rather disappointing...

She submitted it to no less than ten more publishers, all of whom rejected it. The book had by now been doing the rounds for over three years.

At last she gave up. In the next few years there were great changes in her life: her first illness, her move to Balcombe Street after Hilary went to Finstock, the International African Institute's move to High Holborn, and her eventual retirement. But even before the last rejections of *The Sweet Dove Died*, Barbara is making notes about characters that will later be used in *Quartet in Autumn*.

After the publication of *Quartet in Autumn* in 1977 and its appearance on the Booker Prize shortlist, it was a *very* different story. Macmillan, who had published *Quartet,* were very eager for more of her work. James Wright, who had said a few years before that he hoped someone would have the courage to publish *The Sweet Dove Died,* finally did so himself.

> Just back from a holiday in Wessex. It was marvellous to find *The Sweet Dove* waiting. I am on the last few pages of *Excellent Women* which I am enjoying immensely. May I be allowed to finish it? I used to be told to eat up the first course before I was allowed any pudding. The present case is, of course, quite different, because the first course is so delicious.

Macmillan negotiated a deal with Scientia Brombergs in Sweden for an advance of £1000 against royalties. Barbara refused their invitation to the launch party in Sweden – 'It is not at all the kind of thing I like doing.'

Later, in James's absence, his secretary wrote,

> Congratulations on going to no. 3 on the *Sunday Times* bestseller list! We shall all listen avidly to your *Desert Island Discs*…James didn't have time to tell you before he went away that Hatchard's repeated 100 copies of *Sweet Dove* – a phenomenally large number. No wonder you are on the best-seller list.

The Sweet Dove Died was published in June 1978 and reviewed in all the major London newspapers. A reviewer in *The Guardian,* on 1 July 1978 summarised the story in this extraordinary way:

> Miss Pym sets the genteelly desperate love-and-power struggle of *The Sweet Dove Died* in an antique shop where the *feline middle-aged proprietress* [emphasis added] cleverly keeps at bay the admirers of her pretty young male assistant.

Oh, well – we know the *Guardian* often makes mistakes – but can't they read?

Several days later, however, Norman Shrapnel wrote in the same paper a critical review, managing to make only one *Grauniad*-type slip:

> With *The Sweet Dove Died* Barbara Pym converts her scene (no
> trouble at all) from an aura of Anglican churches to one of an-
> tique shops, in a sense their legitimate successors. The uncle
> and nephew who run the establishment our heroine is inter-
> ested in could almost be regarded as vicar and curate – though
> young James, admittedly, would be a bit of a handful in any
> community, with his primly attractive nature and his bisexual
> inclinations. Laura[sic!] is an elegant middle-aged huntress who
> gives point to the ominous Keats title by keeping the young
> man in a flat at the top of her house. It is hard to hate or even
> fear her as much as she seems to deserve; even a touch of sym-
> pathy could break in!

Another reviewer who doesn't appear to have read the text very closely,
Mary Sullivan, describes Leonora in the *Sunday Telegraph* as

> …a handsome woman of a certain age, independent means,
> and exquisite taste; she is also a piranha fish. With a couple of
> lightning strikes she wipes out both Phoebe and Ned, rivals for
> the rather feeble affections of her young friend James…The
> scale is small, the activities genteel; every character is utterly
> self-absorbed…a coldly funny book.

Well, of course she didn't wipe out Ned with a lightning strike, or indeed in any way – he backed himself out.

The Times reviewer had the following views on Leonora and James:

> …idle, cold and exquisite Leonora, of a certain age, who wants
> the adoration of men, but only as lapdogs for her self-
> esteem…[James,] an amazingly wet and epicene young man
> just down from Oxford, who is vaguely learning about antiques
> in his uncle's fashionable antique shop…

Francis King thought the book 'triumphantly back on form', but Peter
Ackroyd, writing in the *Sunday Times* was not entirely uncritical. Another dissenting voice was quoted in an article in *Bookseller*:

> It had, I suppose, to happen. The 'Barbara Pym Lives' move-
> ment had been so powerful last year that it was not surprising

that when her next novel appeared there should be some clever dick declaring 'It would have been kinder to have left Barbara Pym unrediscovered.' The user of that horrid word was Paul Ableman, and he was writing in *The Spectator* about *The Sweet Dove Died*. And he went on in much the same vein: 'The publication of this slight romance, written in a virtually unbroken sequence of genteel clichés, can only tarnish a reputation that was beginning to acquire at least the patina of affectionate nostalgia…Indeed there is hardly enough substance here to fill a medium-length short story in a woman's magazine. It is as if the rude stuff of life were simply too coarse for Leonora's refined soul. *The Sweet Dove Died* contains no hint, no fleeting allusion, to politics, or science, or art (except as décor) or the guilty truth of relationships or anything else that concerns real people in the real world. With one notable exception: the one topic dealt with by Miss Pym that has a counterpart in reality is *class*.

The Times Literary Supplement said 'Leonora is nearly fifty and has a telling way with scarves and scent…'

Gay News, The Listener, and *The Daily Telegraph* all had something to say, but Auberon Waugh in the *Evening Standard* really went to town, with an amusing and generally favourable review on 15 August 1978.

After a few false starts I decided to leave Barbara Pym's new novel The Sweet Dove Died for holiday reading.

Her account of the tribulations of a prosperous middle-aged London spinster who drops her inverted commas and italics around as other women drop paper handkerchiefs – 'It was obvious that Harold was not of their "class"'; 'for she had never enjoyed that kind of thing' – did not seem to belong to the London of rush hour tube trains, sexy cinemas and exciting foreign faces which we all know and love. It was something to be savoured in the delightful cool of the Mediterranean evening, with a glass of some aromatic, little known, aperitif. Or, alternatively, to be thrown into the waste paper basket…

BAM – it worked.

At first I read with mixed irritation and disbelief. Miss Leonora

Eyre, middle-aged, but beautifully preserved, is taken over
queer at Sotheby's after buying a book of Victorian flower illus-
trations, and is rescued by a middle-aged man and his nephew,
James, a young man of attractive looks and pleasing manners. It
is only after twenty pages or so that one appreciates how Miss
Pym has got her knife into this unfortunate lady.

All Miss Pym's characters are silly – the wet young man of inde-
terminate sexual orientation, the pompous uncle, the tiresome
neighbour who keeps cats as a cure for loneliness, the other
lonely friend who mothers a homosexual for company – and
many of them are odious.

But as the full extent of her heroine's ruthless selfishness becomes apparent, one finds that irritation with Miss Pym's
mannered style and precious habits begins to give way to admiration. By the end we even begin to pity the monster she has
created...

Miss Eyre, who collects beautiful and perfect objects, takes a
fancy to the wet young man and immediately exerts herself to
capture him. First she must extricate him from the snares of a
young woman in jeans called Phoebe. James visits Phoebe in a
country cottage where, after a bedroom scene, Phoebe says
'Oh, James, what did we do?' She might well ask, but unless I
am much mistaken I think I know what they did. If so, this is
most unusual, but Leonora, who has spent so many years unat-
tached – one could almost but not quite say untouched – soon
puts a stop to whatever it was.

Next James takes up with a homosexual American called Ned.
In fact, I am not sure that Americans are ever called Ned, just
as I am sure that Leonora would not drink Sauternes with avo-
cado and shrimp, but Miss Pym can't be expected to get
everything right.

Ned is every bit as selfish and ruthless as Leonora, and crueller.
He smashes up this nauseating relationship between the spinster and the wet young man, but because he is so much nastier
than she is, we find our sympathies engaged for the first time.

If one reads the book carefully one discovers from various
oblique clues that it is set in the period 1963/64 when such

people might just have still been around. Anyone who lives now as Leonora lived then would have to be very rich. Such innocence could no longer exist in Central London, even if it ever could. But Miss Pym opens a little shutter on the modern world with her acceptance of homosexual relationships and her terrified peep into the bedroom of Vine Cottage when Phoebe lets her jeans down…an excellent book for reading on holiday.

But after it appeared, James Wright wrote to Barbara 'Auberon Waugh is of course the silliest man alive; even so, he can't help granting you grudging respect.'

The Provincial press was represented, notably by *The Yorkshire Post*, *The Northern Echo*, *The Scotsman*, the *Bath & West Evening Chronicle*, and the *Oxford Mail's* Jayne Gilman:

Leonora…does not at first appear admirable. She is a very nice lady, always beautifully dressed with exquisite taste and such sensitivity. Because Leonora finds physical contact so…distasteful, she likes her admirers to be elderly and past it…James's uncle Humphrey is such a civilized man, with such taste.…James himself is another kettle of fish. Young, insecure, not actually terribly civilized. He has only just realized, for instance, that making lamps out of Chianti bottles is rather laughably bourgeois.

I liked the review in *New Fiction*, July 1978:

The heroine of Barbara Pym's brilliantly readable and amusing new novel is a lady of private means who wears a green chiffon dress in order to savour her crème de menthe to the full. She is good with her house plants, thinks all taxi drivers 'sweet,' considers the comforts of tea-drinking vulgar, and the use of paraffin in the home ill-informed. She admits no object into her London house that is not flawless, and her attitude to the possibility of possessing such a thing as a bucket is not unlike that of Lady Bracknell's daughter confronting the remote Platonic prospect of a spade. Indeed, in many ways, Leonora Eyre is Wilde's Gwendolyn Fairfax surviving, alone and exquisitely middle-aged, into the 1970s. Which is to say that she is also an absolute cow and a pain in the ass.

I had never read Miss Pym before and approached her work with caution following her spectacular rescue from obscurity by Lord David Cecil and Anthony Powell [sic!] last year. My caution was conquered at once by the stylish and flowing rhythm of the narrative, by the oblique wit and stern affection she applies to maddening and impossible people.

Barbara was also having an impact at the other end of the world. In November, a reviewer in *The Age* (Melbourne) wrote:

I hadn't heard of Barbara Pym until the other day when I read an ecstatic review of the seventh novel, *Quartet in Autumn*, in *Time* magazine. The circle of her admirers should be considerably widened with the publication of her eighth novel *The Sweet Dove Died.*

It is a comedy of the highest order and the greatest simplicity. Its appeal should not be limited by the narrowness of its social setting (a quasi intellectual corner of the English middle class). For this novel is placed psychologically in the limitless territory of love and hostility, possessiveness and jealousy…its plot and portraiture achieve a beautiful clarity that is at once bold and subtle. The writing is graceful but plain, almost dead-pan at times. On a few pages the wit is rather crudely underlined, but not often enough to destroy the harmonious shapeliness of this fascinating and satisfying novel.

And David Rowbotham in the *Brisbane Courier* on 23 December 1978 writes indignantly,

The London reviewer Francis Wyndham recently spoke of 'the years of neglect' to which Barbara Pym had been subjected; which is one way of explaining why her name has hardly penetrated to the Antipodes.

Her publishers still do not help much, apart from publishing her latest novel *The Sweet Dove Died*. No photograph of this exceptionally fine English author appears on the dust jacket and no biography except a mean snippet informing the world at large that she lives in Oxfordshire.

Her publishing history has been *appalling*. Between 1950 and 1961 she published 6 novels. Critics and readers preferred Muriel Spark, Iris Murdoch, Penelope Mortimer, and Edna O'Brien, compared with whose styles the style of Pym probably seemed too plain. Pym was not a 'star' or was never given star treatment. Not surprisingly the woman fell silent. Only now has she taken up the pen again, and now is being acclaimed, at last, as a major English novelist. This new novel alone is enough to show how wrongly, and wretchedly, she has been previously disregarded.

She is one of those rarest of authors: a master of the ordinary. Although all but one of the characters in this novel are English, they all seem essentially universal in their value and validity no matter how very English they appear. And on superficial examination the story in which they are involved can seem so trite. On deeper examination it can be seen to be momentous to them: a story of daily lives, of loves, of loss, of age and youth, of generations past, and of generations doomed to pass. All of this…is manifested in apparently the most undramatic of happenings…This is a *marvellous* novel.

When *The Sweet Dove Died* was published in the United States in 1979, only *Quartet in Autumn* and a reprint of *Excellent Women* had appeared there previously. A number of prestigious American journals as well as some small-town publications reviewed it. While most of the English reviews, as well as the Australian, were favourable, in the United States there were good and bad reviews in almost equal number. Taking the good reviews first, Walter Clemons wrote in *Newsweek* on 16 April 1979:

> When *Excellent Women* and *Quartet in Autumn* – her first novel in 16 years – appeared here last year, I didn't rush to try them. That an author's name rhymes with 'prim' and that her subjects, churchgoing spinsters and lonely office workers facing retirement, didn't sound very peppy, are not good excuses but those were mine.
>
> Her eighth novel has not only converted me but made me hunt up and read the other two with amazed pleasure…*The Sweet*

Dove Died is lethally funny and subtly very pronouncedly sensual to a degree new in Pym's work...This is a brilliant perfect piece of work.

Polly Brodie, in the American *Library Journal* of 15 March 1979 said,

In this second novel since the 16-year silence, Pym again anatomises loneliness. *The Sweet Dove Died* is on a smaller scale than *Quartet in Autumn* but its exposure of the private traps of emotional solipsism is no less lucid. Leonora Eyre (the echoes of Fidelio and Jane Eyre are deliberate and ironic) is an elegant, exquisite ageing woman who loves Victorian bibelots and allows herself to be collected by an antique dealer and his young nephew. Leonora is presented with a coolness that keeps one from really liking her, but the analysis of her inability to love or be loved forces the reader to examine his or her own heart. Sophisticated entertainment.

A reviewer in *Reconnaissance,* Jan 1979 declared that

It isn't the plot of a Pym which matters, it's the flavour, and here we have a quiet, elegant, richly comic book – not of the ha-ha but of the involuntary snort type – about Leonora, who is an 'older woman' to James, but an object of desire to his uncle. There are the irritating infiltrations into their relationships by a bold young American, Nick [sic], and a very gauche girl, Phoebe. Barbara Pym's work is that of a miniaturist, so get your sights suitably adjusted and you may find what you see extremely rewarding...

Mildred Zaiman in *The Hartford Courant* predicted that 'It is highly probable that the novels of Ms Pym with their impeccable artistry and the economy of means will long outlast many of today's best sellers.' And *Tulsa Home & Garden* said unequivocally, 'She is quite simply one of the best novelists writing in England today.'

There were mixed reactions from Cyndi Meagher in *Detroit News*:

The Sweet Dove Died has little of the romantic suspense of *Excellent Women,* nor the important concerns of *Quartet in Autumn*. It is not quite as much fun as the first, nor quite so intriguing as the second. But, perhaps like one of Humphrey's fine porcelains, its excellence provides great pleasure. And its wit is delightfully wicked.

And Penny Pinkham in the *Boston Sunday Globe* thought that 'Pym's latest missed something':

> *The Sweet Dove Died* is a perfectly controlled performance of a high order of skill, intelligent, crystal-faceted, distanced. It is the distancing that ultimately robs the book of the power of its execution. We are peering through an ironic prism, somehow bereft of the light source that would let it blaze away...Barbara Pym is a writer to admire but not, judging from this book, one to love. One to pursue, though; there are rare skills here.

Several reviewers were frankly disappointed, *Kirkus Reviews*, for one:

> In *Excellent Women* and *Quartet in Autumn* Pym managed to invest ordinary, nearly pathetic English lives with an ironic dignity and offbeat charm. Here, however, her economical narrative edge still slices marvellously. Pym's people are simply difficult to believe and impossible to like... perhaps part of the problem is that the characters here are of a better class than most of Pym's other frail heroes: class and taste are certainly the preoccupations of handsomely mature Leonora Eyre – a worldly but prim unmarried lady of leisure who is in fact frozen at a schoolgirl stage of emotional and sexual development. We watch as she quickly develops an obsessive romantic/platonic attachment to dreamy young James – nephew and assistant of a London antique dealer whose attentions Leonora flirtatiously invites and then repels...When James, a fellow of flexibly nebulous sexuality, is revealed to have a chippy in the suburbs, Leonora displaces her and induces James to move into a gorgeous flat in her own smart house. But James's *new* lover, canny and smarmy American Ned, is more than a match for Leonora and steals James completely away...If these people were a bit more substantial, the novel might work as a parable of possessive love's destructiveness...But as it is, Pym gives us only a sad, rather superficial story of high-toned misfits.

The *Chattanooga* Times:

> The story is about an aging lady who latches on to a considerably younger man and the competition she meets from male and female alike. It's a less interesting story than I seem to be making it sound. And it discomforts me to make negative noises about a book many others are getting enthusiastic about. Still, I did find the characters unappealing and the story affected.

And a final putdown, this from the *Worcester* [Massachusetts] *Telegram:*

> If *The Sweet Dove Died* is any indication of the ongoing quality of Ms Pym's heralded autumnal renaissance, she may enjoy a short-lived revival indeed. There is a gaping void at the core of this book. It is not the usual British priggishness either, so noticeable to American readers, but a much more elementary lack of human vitality. The characters are simply unable to generate any respect, sympathy or interest. Leonora is a soulless and icy vamp...James is a dullard and a bore.

Friends and fans across the world wrote in, of course. Most were women and few offered any critical analysis, simply mentioning the characters they liked best, or merely saying how much they had enjoyed the latest work of one of their favourite authors. However, it is interesting to see what impressed some 'ordinary' readers.

> I would like to tell you how very much I enjoyed reading your book *The Sweet Dove Died*...what I particularly like about your work is the way you depict single people, that disappearing breed to which I belong...

> Since I have just finished *The Sweet Dove Died* I felt moved (unusually, not a habit) to write to you...My mother first introduced me to your writing in the 50s, when I 'graduated' to adult literature. No other book has given me more pleasure than one of yours...I hope the detachment with which you appeared to produce *The Sweet Dove Died* is with you still, and there is more to come...

> *The Sweet Dove Died* – I found it unremittingly enjoyable and the characters fascinating. For myself, possibly James tops the bill – I have never read a more penetrating analysis of bi-

sexuality, yet at the same time so wittily done.

Sybil Birch, a clergyman's wife, wrote

> Leonora worried me a bit. I couldn't believe that she would read *In Memoriam* on a train, or in bed, or, in fact, anywhere. She doesn't seem up to it – I think I would have given her *Vogue* or *Good Housekeeping*, or a 'nice' novel.
>
> And would Leonora, so self-centred, calculating and frigid, ever have been to bed with any one? It's practically impossible to imagine she could unbend to that extent. However, I did enjoy the book. I'm afraid though that you rather shocked Sylvia Midgeley. She didn't like it. I'm pretty sure it was the homosexual element, as her brother with whom she lives has always been that way inclined (no scandal, but *very* fond of boys, and so a worry to my husband regarding the choir boys.)

Elsie Miller, a friend, said, 'I found *The Sweet Dove Died* fascinating. It doesn't glow for me as *Quartet* does, though it has more overt comedy.' Elsie lent her copy to a mutual friend, Helen MacGregor, a publisher's reader.

> Gosh, Barbara! What an absolutely *glorious* novel. Elsie Miller bought *The Sweet Dove Died*, and knowing what a Pymite I've been for aeons, gave me, as they say in my native Argyllshire, 'the lend' of it. As *The Times* review pointed out, the characters are in the main not the kind of whom one would want to make one's Dearest Friend, but oh, don't I know them all. Very few writers have your flair for 'multum in parvo' and the subtlety of managing to make Ned one of the most genuinely *evil* men in fiction without going into any details – just innuendo. The one character for whom I felt genuinely sorry because she *was* hurt, was Phoebe – she was young and vulnerable, and though well rid of James, scarred. It is the *writing*, though, as well as the devilishly clever characterisation – only a skilled technician could be so deceptively simple.

Trixie Walsh in Edinburgh reported on the proceedings of the previous night's meeting of the Edinburgh University Wives Book Circle:

> People were noting that your '78 productions are considerably

less 'innocent' than your early work, but it was appreciated that you still left things for the imagination to work on. I must say that although I could never love the book as I do *Excellent Women*, yet *The Sweet Dove Died* strikes me as your major work. It is quite horribly good. You've not touched on pure evil before, and Ned is wholly convincing. We can bear him because he only does harm to the shallow James and the abominable Leonora, and both of these characters one is glad to see done down.

Tom Cole from Baltimore wrote,

> I ordered *The Dove* May 31st at one of my local bookshops, got it on June 5 and read it right away…I've already loaned my copy to four-five friends who have delighted in it. I too was delighted with it. At first I felt it wouldn't work – the lean, very sketchy exposition of your tale…but indeed it does work, the story takes fire, and the style proved appropriate, though not the gently witty or leisurely style of the earlier novels. There is a bit of Mrs Gray in Leonora, not an altogether likeable character …she may be defeated by Ned, but she'll not cry uncle or change her style. But you do share a certain irony and style with Henry James…I have just read James's *The Reverberator*, and the concise, direct, sharp, unrelenting wit is very like your novel…

And Ellie Smith of Chestnut Hill, Massachusetts, said 'I agree with everything complimentary that is said about your most recent book *The Sweet Dove Died*. It is a treasure.'

But of all the accolades received for *The Sweet Dove Died* the one which Barbara may have found most amusing, touching even, was from Cyril Clemens, a distant cousin of Samuel Langhorne Clemens himself and editor of the *Mark Twain Journal*, in a very badly typed and laid-out letter on its Society's notepaper, which read:

Dear Barbara Pym

In recognition of
your outstanding contribution to literature by your

THE SWEET DOVE DIED

you have been unanimously elected

A DAUGHTER OF MARK TWAIN

An earlier version of this paper was presented at the 2007 Annual General Meeting in Oxford.

12

From Four Point Turn *to* Quartet in Autumn

1973 – 1977

Have thought of an idea for a novel, based on our
office move – all old crabby characters,
petty and obsessive, bad tempered – how easily one
of them could have a false breast!

From Four Point Turn *to* Quartet in Autumn

On 22 April 1971 Barbara was diagnosed with breast cancer, particularly bad timing as Hilary was away on an extended visit to Greece and could not be contacted. But Barbara's other friends were supportive and she did not have to wait long for treatment.

Her 1971 pocket diary has the following entries:

April 22. Lump
April 27. Hospital [St Mary's, Paddington]
April 28. In hospital
April 29. Operation
May 20. Go home
June 10. Hospital for bra
October 26. Hospital

Barbara made a good recovery and returned to work at the IAI in the summer. St Dunstan's Chambers, part of a redevelopment area, was due to be demolished, so the Institute moved to High Holborn. Barbara much regretted that Gamages was also to be demolished, but told Bob Smith,

Of course, the new place will be more convenient – nearer to the British Museum, SOAS [London University's School of Oriental and African Studies], Bourne and Hollingsworth [a departmental store not unlike Gamages], Marks and Spencer and other desirable places.

Hilary, having retired from the BBC, bought Barn Cottage in the little village of Finstock, near Oxford, in 1972, and Barbara secured a room for weekdays in a friend's house in Balcombe Street, near Marylebone Station, going to Finstock for the weekends.

Barbara always wrote of what she knew. She got a completely new view of the world when she was ill – hospital waiting rooms, doctors' surgeries, fellow patients. Of course she would have to write a book about them.

In her notebook for early 1972, Barbara gave her first intimation of a new novel, based on this recent episode in her life, and partly on the move of the IAI to Holborn:

> Have thought of an idea for a novel, based on our office move – all old crabby characters, petty and obsessive, bad tempered – how easily one of them could have a false breast! But I'd better not write it till I have time to concentrate on it (look what happened to the last).

However, as she later wrote to Philip Larkin, 'I am writing, quietly in bed in the early morning, a novel about four people in their sixties working in the same office,' and in her notebook for 1972-3 there are many notes for this novel, many of which may have been gleaned from overhearing in a hospital setting the conversations of lonely women dependent on the welfare state.

> A lonely person found dead with no food in the house. A cultured woman who has worked in an office – who realises that she is in danger but is too late to stop herself.

> There could be talk in the office about elderly people being found dead with no food in the house. One might have a tin of soup but lack the strength to open it.

> I have fallen through the net of the welfare state, she thought, picturing this more as a coarse, serviceable hair net than a net to catch trapeze artists should they fall.

> A great deal of strange food is eaten in this office because none of the older staff can afford to go out to lunch.

> The beginning of her rejection and slipping through the net. She looks out of her window and sees a rather bright woman coming up to the door – pretends she isn't in.

> We are trying to visit at least once a fortnight all the lonely ones – those who live alone I mean. I suppose it's not quite the

same thing, she said doubtfully.

She could get 'flu the week nobody came.

All right? Are you all right? A nice voice and a pleasant blurry face with anxious grey eyes. 'I'm going,' she thought, 'slipping through the net of the welfare state.'

Nobody caring – she had come to that, accepted it with courage, brave, facing it, repeating to herself: no husband, no child, no brother, no sister, no friend. Quite alone.

Perhaps in my novel the two women retire (at 60) and the men don't (waiting to be 65).

The friend in the country marries a clergyman some years younger than herself. Letty reading the letter from Marjorie.

Letty the pensioner – not a fragile old lady but hard up none-the-less.

Angry little Norman in Lincoln's Inn Fields – angry at the semi-nudity of the young women and the long flowing hair of the men – angry at the older men watching the girls playing netball, at people sucking iced lollies and cornets.

Barbara suffered other health problems about that time, and she made many visits to the hospital and to her doctor in 1974. In March she had a slight stroke, caused by excessive calcium in the blood, which led to a temporary inability to read or write properly. She received treatment at the Radcliffe Hospital in Oxford throughout April. On recovery she was told she must retire. Daryll Forde had died the year before, no successor had been found, and the Institute's work was changing, so she was probably glad to leave and reside permanently in the country.

In her 1973-4 notebook, Barbara included many more notes, rather more specific than those in the previous notebook:

> Shortage of milk bottles. Marcia has milk bottles in her garden shed – a hangover from the end of the war – 'No bottle, no milk – only fair, isn't it?' the slogan.
>
> If only, Letty thought, Christianity could have had a British, even an English, origin! Palestine was so remote.
>
> Norman would rejoice at the sight of a mutilated motor car -

its side bashed in.

Norman has always had 'difficult hair' – bristly and cut very short. A slight hint of the pudding basin, when younger, mediaeval page.

Letty – soft faded blonde hair worn rather too long. How lucky you are not to have gone grey, friends said. But she knew that there was white among the blonde, silver threads among the gold.

Marcia had dark stiff lifeless hair which she had always dyed herself in the bathroom since she was 35 and had first started to go grey. Rolled up at the back.

The net of the welfare state and the social services was closing in around them. Yet, in a curious way, since a net however tightly drawn still had holes, Letty and Marcia were to fall through it.

For each of the characters a visit to the public library – the head librarian, his golden hair hanging to his shoulders. Eric [Edgar] would be looking people up in *Crockford* or occasionally *Who's Who* or *Who Was Who*. He didn't care much for reading.

Letty – a novel, but weren't as nice as they used to be, so it had to be biography.

Norman – a place to sit and read the papers. Marcia the same. She might leave milk bottles there and with her obsession about saving electricity it might be a place of warmth and light. Pamphlets about services for old people etc.

The earliest draft of part of the novel appears to begin as a diary of Barbara's stay in hospital in 1971, with the following revealing entry:

Obviously one falls a little for one's surgeon. How easily might some lonely slightly deranged spinster carry this passion to unnatural and embarrassing lengths, going to his home, sending him presents etc.

The surgeon would, of course, be used to women falling for him.

No doubt Barbara remembered her own youthful feelings for her Oxford tutors, and how she used to follow them secretly.

A very rough handwritten draft, as usual on rectos only, with comments and amendments on versos, is dated 23 April 1973 at Finstock. It is an early draft with the names of the characters not yet established, e.g. Letty/Rose, Norman/Neville, Edmund/Eric/Edgar.

There is another handwritten rough partial draft in a thin exercise book dated 17 June 1974, and another two with mainly typed drafts of various passages. There is no completed, publication-ready, draft.

With all her medical treatment from 1971 and then throughout 1976 – Barbara records in her diary for that year at least four visits to the hospital and many more to her doctor in Long Hanborough – she had plenty of opportunity to observe the ailing, the lonely, and those 'slipping through the net of the welfare state.'

> Apr 14. Finished typing novel, 131pp.
> Oct 22. Sent novel to Hamish Hamilton
> Nov 8. Novel back from H.H.

In her notebook for 1976 Barbara writes on 13 December 1976,

> Writing to Pamela Hansford Johnson to tell her that Hamish Hamilton had already rejected my novel (*Four Point Turn*) when he had just written to her saying that he was 'eager to read it.'

But 1977 was to be a very different year, after her endorsement as an 'underrated' author in the TLS on 21 January. Her diary thereafter is crammed with entries resounding with success and appreciation:

> Jan 21. 'BP in TLS'. Paul Binding and Philip Larkin rang.
> Jan 24. BP on Radio Oxford
> Feb 2. Sent 'Last Quartet' to Macmillan

On 7 February Barbara records in her notebook

> The novel (*Last Quartet*) has arrived at Macmillan and the girl who acknowledges it addresses me as Mrs Pym. This puts me into a different category altogether!

On 14 February

> Alan Maclean rang from Macmillan saying that they would *love* to publish the novel (*Four Point Turn* or *Last Quartet*, whatever it is called). Can hardly believe it can be true but he said he would confirm by letter.

The diary continues:

> Feb 21. Alan Maclean [Macmillan] rang
>
> Mar 3. Lunch with Alan Maclean and James Wright. They like *Quartet in Autumn* [as a title] – a sort of compromise...
>
> Apr 18. Posted *The Sweet Dove Died* to Macmillan
>
> Apr 28. Proofs [of *Q in A*] came.
>
> May 4. Posted proofs to Macmillan
>
> May 19. Tea with Lord David [Cecil]
>
> Jun 24. BBC2 Film [*Tea with Miss Pym*]
>
> Aug 22. Monica Cunningham, Macmillan publicity, rang
>
> Sep 14. Radio Oxford 4.pm
>
> Sep 15. *Q in A* (Macmillan) published. *Excellent Women* and *A Glass of Blessings* (Cape) reissued

Hazel Holt says that Philip Larkin sent her an enormous congratulations card, inside which he had drawn a dragon, labelled 'Maschler', pierced to the heart by a spear[1]. This card is among Barbara's papers.

> Oct 3. Someone from Macmillan rang re *The Sweet Dove Died* proofs.
>
> Oct 18. John Julius [John Julius Cooper, 2nd Viscount Norwich, usually known as John Julius Norwich, a historian and TV personality], Macmillans and BBC
>
> Oct 21. Book Programme [*Tea with Miss Pym*]
>
> Nov 1. BBC TV Centre [to see the programme again with the producer and Robert Robinson]

In October Barbara's success was triumphantly crowned when *Quartet in Autumn* was short-listed for the Booker prize. Philip Larkin was the chief judge. She attended the prize-giving dinner on 23 November, where among many leading lights of the literary and arts world, she met for the first time Tom Maschler ('charming, of course!').[2]

Quartet in Autumn was received enthusiastically by the press, though Jeremy Treglown in the *New Statesman* on 23 September 1977 made this snide comment:

> One of the good things about *Quartet in Autumn* is that for once Barbara Pym's characters don't spend much time casting about for appropriate literary quotations.

Lotus Snow, in her essay 'Literary Allusions in the Novels', offered an explanation:

> Conceivably [Treglow] has overlooked the obvious reason for this: whereas the characters of the other novels are persons of culture, the foursome in *Quartet in Autumn* are office workers of average education.[3]

Paul Bailey, writing in the *Observer* on 25 September 1977 suggested that

> The publication of Barbara Pym's first novel in 16 years marks the return of a considerable stylist, whose quietly accomplished work has been shamefully neglected...it is a sad comedy of the small preoccupations of everyday life.
>
> The four principal characters...have loneliness in common...but that's an appalling fact none of them gives much more than a passing thought to...Q in A is not gloomy in tone, however. The ghastly implications are kept in check by Barbara Pym's subtle appreciation of the comic aspects of her people's lives...small in scale, Q in A is on its own terms an exquisite, even magnificent, work of art.

As Barbara wrote to Bob Smith, although the *Church Times* did not usually review novels [perhaps a fairly recent decision, because it had reviewed most of Barbara's earlier works], the editor said that he would this time 'if only because I have given so many splendid free commercials for the *Church Times*'.

Quartet in Autumn, set in the present, is obviously by the same hand [as *Excellent Women* and *A Glass of Blessings*] but with a sombre sense of the sere and yellow. Edwin, Marcia, Letty and Norman are colleagues sharing some unskilled office work and all approaching retirement. They live alone and are virtually friendless, but have evolved their own routine for getting by.

A more sophisticated, thematic approach has replaced the earlier narrative style – four strings each contributing its own peculiar strain in a technically harmonious whole. But it all seems more than a generation removed from the 50s, when four-letter words, long-haired curates in jeans, or rowdy Nigerian neighbours would have been inconceivable. Even the ecclesiastical interest is significantly subdued.

The keen eye is as acute as ever, though the humour is a little sadder…there is an unmistakeable touch of frost where earlier there had been sunshine.

Dear Miss Pym, may your volumes increase. But if your characters are inexorably going to age, perhaps they may be permitted some sort of second childhood so that we may go on smiling with you.

Philip Larkin contributed to the *Observer*'s 'Books of the Year' on 18 December 1977.

Most people will know the story of Barbara Pym by now, but where *Quartet in Autumn* differs from the six 1950s novels is in its macabre portrait of self-starving Marcia, one of her four characters facing retirement with courage and the inimitable BP humour. Cheers for Miss Pym's return although as the general (as distinct from the publisher's) reader knows, she never really went away.

Beryl Bainbridge was another contributor to this column:

Quartet in Autumn by Barbara Pym, a beautifully sparse account of four elderly people nearing retirement in Britain's Welfare State; funny and sad.

Jilly Cooper was a third:

Barbara Pym's gentle, slyly comic novels with their vicars and mildly bickering parish ladies always remind me of Jane Austen let loose in Cranford. An addict since my teens, I must recommend *Quartet in Autumn*...which traces the lonely though sometimes defiant lives of four people working in the same office on the brink of retirement. The comedy is bleaker...but the compassion for human vanities, and the gift for the unexpected are still undiminished.

The book was also well received overseas. The Melbourne *Age* said on 10 February 1978:

Her recently republished *Excellent Women* is a gem of social comedy but *Quartet in Autumn* is quieter, less quizzical, as though in the intervening ten years pity and sympathy have finally overwhelmed auctorial detachment.

Publishers' Weekly (USA) on 24 July 1978 was also favourable:

No doubt about it [BP] is an accomplished writer, and American critics and readers will find her pure gold. [In Q in A] she explores the lives of four aging office workers on the verge of retirement. Nothing much has ever happened to any of them, nor is it apt to. As each single voice states its melancholy, lonely theme, intertwines and interacts with the others through all the small details and little tensions of office life, a quiet portrait of an almost on-the-shelf society emerges. But though the harmony is in a minor key, the melody is one of beauty, dignity and spirit as these voices, unnoticed by the world, sing on.

The *Chicago Tribune Book World* of 10 January 1978 thought

Quartet in Autumn is a small masterpiece, beautifully composed, and the most pungent work I've read about a group of aging people since Muriel Spark's classic *Memento Mori*. The autumnal quartet are uneasily bound to one another through shared work space, the default of empty and barely used private lives, and their common apprehension about imminent retirement

Shirley Hazzard also found a comparison with *Memento Mori:*

Quartet in Autumn moves within a smaller compass than

Muriel Spark's *Memento Mori*, which treats a similar theme; and Miss Pym is poignant where Miss Spark is masterly. But this is fine, durable stuff, with an originality that, however you approach it, gives back the truth.

But, as I have said before, there is no pleasing everyone. Here is Marjorie Bilker in the Milwaukee *Journal*, 24 September 1978:

This tight-lipped tale presents the lives of two men and two women on the brink of retirement...I found it hard to identify with the characters and circumstances of the story, which seems in a way to unfold on a planet light years away.

Friends wrote in, as usual. Barbara had sent a draft of the book to Robert Smith a couple of months before publication. He had written to her on 29 July1976,

Dearest Barbara

I finished *Four Point Turn* in bed this morning between 5 and 6 am...it was compelling reading. It's a short book, and in a way one wouldn't have it longer because as a study in 'retirement' it has its almost unbearable side. I think the decline of Marcia is very well done indeed. The other three main characters are equally alive. I think you have lighted upon a new theme – or at least added a new dimension to the theme which gave originality to your other books. 'They' would be silly not to publish it.

Edwin seems the only one of the quartet with any purpose in life...Norman comes to life, but is nevertheless rather neglected – I'd have liked a bit more of him. And at 59/60, surely both Letty and Marcia seem far too old.

He wrote again when he received a complimentary copy:

I do want to thank you so much for my copy of *Quartet*. I read it immediately you left. It's very good, but I had not realised how different it is from your other books, being so much darker in tone. The effect is rather frightening, despite the relief provided by acute observation of amusing trivia. The social worker and the woman next door are dreadfully well done. I wonder now what the critics will make of it. I think that in one sense – perhaps the most important one – it's your best book, and yet I don't look forward to re-reading it, whereas I re-read your others all the time.

Robert Liddell wrote very soon after the book was published:

I got back from Italy two days ago to find your letter and the book…I think the novel is remarkably fine – it is like *Excellent Women* twenty years on, so to speak. And though we are still in the land of Pym there are deeper tones…I began the book hoping for more familiar themes and people – but I do admire the progress and development it shows…I shouldn't be surprised if the Quartet were not your greatest novel to date.

And he read it some months later 'with increased pleasure and admiration.'

Evelyn Forde, a medical doctor and widow of Daryll Forde, the late Director of the IAI, wrote:

Dear Barbara

Your new novel has given me enormous pleasure. The description of Marcia's one-sided relationship to hospital and doctor was so accurate and sympathetic that even though I spend my working life detached from the illnesses and miseries of the sick, it brought tears to my eyes – but then I, like you, have seen the patient's side.

I admire your ability to weave so much human interaction out of four inarticulate people – sadly I meet them all the time in Willesden too!…

I so wish Daryll could have known about your deserved good fortune – he would have been absolutely delighted even though I suspect Q in A wouldn't have been on his wavelength.

Peggy Makins, an old friend, and agony aunt on *Woman*, who always commented favourably on Barbara's books, wrote,

Quartet I have the greatest respect for. It is remarkable and chilling and horribly true…I doubt if it could ever be *likeable*…it has grim humour, but the loneliness, the withdrawing into one's self, the acute sense of despair – these were an aspect of your insight which made me, at 62, feel the cold of death.

Joyce Tindall, however, had some reservations:

> To be frank, I didn't enjoy this last book as much as the earlier ones.
>
> I felt you had progressed beyond me – rather as modern art progresses beyond my capacity to understand and appreciate. I felt that in concentrating on the fundamental loneliness and independence of older people you had stripped away all the detailed observation of character and odd quirks of behaviour and circumstances which for me make up much of the fascination of your writing – to recognise oneself and one's friends is all part of the fun!

But a fan, Mrs Joan Jones, had no reservations whatsoever:

> Dear Miss Pym
>
> I have just finished reading Q in A and would like to tell you how very much I enjoyed it. The way you built up a picture of the four clerical officers working in a Government building, although you never actually stated this, was a masterly piece of writing.

Mary Lansdale, another fan, was most enthusiastic:

> Dear Miss Pym
>
> I am so happy both for you and for myself. After years of patient longing I shall be able to find delight and refuge in another book of yours. I would gladly sell all that Doris Lessing and Margaret Drabble have written for one of your elegant and enchanting books.

And Ruth Montefiore thought

> … the characters are so real I felt I'd met them. I hope you will write another and another! And it isn't only me – knocking on 60 myself, who enjoyed it – my daughter aged 20 loved it too.

Dorothea Abbott wrote that she

> loved reading *Quartet in Autumn*, but being a *Some Tame Ga-*

zelle fan missed the light-heartedness. By contrast, [a] friend who was at St Hilda's, reckons it's your best book yet.

Angela Barton, from Chesterfield, Derbyshire, said

> Your *Quartet in Autumn* has given me so much pleasure that it would be positively ungrateful not to say thank you.
>
> I read it in two gulps and laughed aloud with delight so often it was well that I was alone It's the sort of book where the characters are so 'right', you keep saying 'Oh, *yes!*' as you read. Not only did some of their little ways remind me of other people, but I chuckled to recognise myself doing Marcia things like hoarding plastic bags...But mostly I found I was doing Edwin things, like snooping round churches to see if they are DSCR [Daily celebration, Sung Eucharist on Sundays, scheduled Confessions, and continuous Reservation of the Blessed Sacrament – the code used in *Mowbray's Church Guide* to denote 'full Catholic privileges']...Thank you once again for the enjoyment I had from *Quartet in Autumn.*

Barbara's old friend Muriel Maby, wrote on 15 May 1978,

> I am very much enjoying *Quartet in Autumn* being read on *Woman's Hour* [BBC radio programme]. It is compulsive listening – a very clever book – a little more clinical perhaps than the earlier ones but one to be very proud of.

Mr. H E Todd, of Berkhamsted, one of the few men to write, said,

> Dear Barbara Pym
>
> This is just to tell you that I have thoroughly enjoyed *Quartet in Autumn.* The characters were with me as I read it. Jane Austen with a soupçon of Kingsley Amis!

Many readers noted the book's sadness; Rosemary Byford, a fan, was

> extremely pleased to read the reviews and reports about *Quartet*...I'm afraid I didn't enjoy it so much because the sadder tone in it echoed some of my feelings as I was about to retire from teaching so felt a bit old and sad myself!

Another thought that

Like other readers I find *Quartet in Autumn* rather sombre. Perhaps it is that life being sombre enough I want a 'nice book' to escape into, and poor Marcia was all too reminiscent of an old aunt of mine.

A third had 'just read *Quartet in Autumn* and thoroughly enjoyed it, though I found it a little sad'.

Several later commentators, who had time for reflection, considered *Quartet in Autumn* Barbara's best novel. Kathy Ackley[4] thought it her masterpiece. Robert Emmet Long suggested that it 'represents a splendid recovery of Pym's powers as a novelist, and is the great triumph of her late period'.[5] And Liddell writes that 'it is darker and sadder than any other of Barbara's novels...but it is her strongest, finest work.'[6]

13

'Grey and Pointed at Both Ends'
The Genesis and Public Reception of A Few Green Leaves

1963 – 1979

When I wrote *Some Tame Gazelle* I didn't know nearly so much about village life as I do now.

13

'Grey and Pointed at Both Ends'

A Few Green Leaves was Barbara's last novel, the first draft of which she completed early in 1979, recording in her diary: 'This afternoon I finished my novel in its first very imperfect draft. May I be spared to retype and revise it, loading every rift with ore!'

Although the book was written over quite a short period (1977-79) just after the publication of *Quartet in Autumn*, the germ of an idea of a 'village' novel was sown much earlier. After the great disappointment of the rejection of *An Unsuitable Attachment* in 1963 and the years that followed, Barbara was dispirited, and wrote: 'What can my notebooks contain except the usual bits and pieces that can never now be worked into fiction.' However, she was not entirely unnerved, and her notebooks do actually reveal that she was working hard on several ideas for a new novel. As she intimated, these notebooks demonstrate little continuity – evidently Barbara jotted down ideas as they came to her, without reference to earlier entries which sometimes contradict the later.

In her notebook covering 1963-8, Barbara envisaged several situations which might be used in her next novel, including a big house; a town woman who has retired to the country; an interregnum at the church – the old vicar had been a gentleman who rode to hounds, the new vicar has his mother with him, or the new vicar has a boyfriend with whom some people had seen him on holiday; hostility of the villagers to newcomers.

Barbara next considers characters: a young woman writer; her 'lover'; her friend from London who comes down for weekends; the vicar of course, his mother/housekeeper/boyfriend; an elderly woman, her present husband; her former husband. Then more situations: the people at the big house; the people going over the house; a cottage on the estate of the big house; people going to the pub.

And it is in this notebook that *fox's droppings* are first mentioned! Where Barbara found the phrase I have not ascertained, but clearly she was determined to use it at some time.

Barbara asked Robert Liddell's advice on the plot. He suggested the following:

> A man (or woman) going into the country to edit the literary remains of a son (or daughter) killed in the war. This plot has been rather often used, but it could certainly provide a pretext for coming into the country and it could then turn out that the woman discovers something about living people nearer at hand, e.g. the vicar who is a kind of relation to the people at the great house.

Barbara did of course use the theme of editing literary remains in *The Sweet Dove Died*. Her next idea was this:

> A man of early middle age, as yet unmarried, buys a house with a woman friend. He has another woman friend, but the two women have never met. Perhaps he is an anthropologist and lunches with his old friend Rupert Stonebird at the RCS [Royal Commonwealth Society]. He has lent furniture to both women. One woman…lives in the country and has to make a special journey up to town to pay a secret visit to the house – or rather to look at it from the outside. In the end the man marries a much younger girl.

And then this:

> The man has been to Lisbon looking at manuscripts, and the woman has been working at the Embassy. They had walked in the Estufa Fria. They might know Piers Longridge.

You may remember that Leonora and an admirer had once walked in the Estufa Fria. You will also remember that Piers grew up in Portugal, and taught Portuguese in London. It is interesting to note how Barbara keeps coming back to her earlier characters.

Next she considers a few names for her characters – this is a little exercise she obviously enjoyed, as it is something she always did when planning her novels: Cecily, Abigail, Julian, Elinor, Rosamund, Dorothea, Leonora, Rose, Marian, Pansy.

After this Barbara starts on a more structured synopsis, drawing on her previous notes:

> There is this man, an antique dealer, whom the country woman, Eleanor, has got to know because his mother (who knows about foxes' droppings) lives in the same village and they have become quite close. He had a flat in town which the town woman Rosamund, packed up for him and put the furniture in storage. But he let Eleanor have some things for her cottage and she went up to the furniture depository in London to choose them, not knowing about the other woman until the man at the furniture repository casually mentions her. Then he [the so-far unnamed antique dealer] comes back from abroad and buys a house…But in the meantime, he has met a young girl, perhaps through his old friend Rupert Stonebird and Rupert's wife Penelope. He has been getting antiques for Rupert's house in NW London.

She has married off Rupert to Penelope Grandison even though *An Unsuitable Attachment* remained unpublished!

The furniture depository episode was partly based on fact; Bob Smith had lent furniture to Barbara without her knowing that he had also lent some to another woman. But in the true life case there was no suggestion of rivalry.

As I'm sure you will have noticed by now, these notes begin to sound like a preparation for *The Sweet Dove Died*, the original version of which was a hybrid between its final version and an early version of *A Few Green Leaves*. In the chapter on *The Sweet Dove Died* I wrote about two drafts of another attempt at a village novel called *Spring*, whose first chapter begins startlingly with Violet Couchman saying 'No, Lionel, a fox's droppings are *grey* and pointed at both ends.'

After *The Sweet Dove Died* was completed in 1968, Barbara spent much time in the ensuing years trying to find a publisher for it, but at the same time she was writing notes about characters she would later use in *Quartet in Autumn*. Rejection never put her off trying again. The 'village' novel was put aside.

After Barbara's rediscovery and the publication of *Quartet in Autumn* and *The Sweet Dove Died*, she turned her thoughts again to her 'country' novel. She had some new ideas now, gleaned from her actual experience of village people, for she had been living permanently in Finstock since 1974. 'When I wrote *Some Tame Gazelle*,' she said, 'I didn't know nearly so much about village life as I do now.'

One event which was based on fact is that apparently on Palm Sunday the local people were allowed to go into Wychwood Forest to collect wood. In the book the date is changed to Low Sunday, one week after Easter. Barbara mentions in her diaries in two consecutive years going into the forest on the feast day, but according to the Forest's website, Leafield villagers are now allowed to enter the forest every Tuesday to collect wood, but 'only as much as one man can carry.' The great house may be loosely based on Cornford Park, Charlbury, a Royal hunting lodge in the 17th century, now an estate owned by a peer but much updated, offering office accommodation, rental properties, and hire of the house and gardens for private events, including a music festival.

Another is the coffee morning scene. In her diary Barbara reports going to a 'Coffee morning in Minster Lovell in aid of the Women's Institute. One man present. The woman who won the bottle of wine in the raffle of course said she never drank it but that she had nothing against those who did like it.'

A third is the umbrella swapping incident, based on this diary entry:

> We went to [the BBC studio in] Bristol where I did a talk for Pamela Howe to be broadcast in *Woman's Hour*. And in the end I got her umbrella and she got mine, not discovered until we were miles apart! This could well provide a ridiculous episode for a novel – Emma meeting Claudia and they got each other's umbrella. How annoyed Claudia would be getting Emma's inferior umbrella.

Barbara's heroine was at first to be 'a young woman recovering from an illness, who had been lent a cottage in the grounds of the great house. She is a writer of historical novels, called Etty, Effie, Emily, or Emma. Had her mother (an English literature academic, possibly a contemporary of Jane Cleveland) named her after Jane Austen's heroine?' But later Barbara says,

> My heroine, Emma – her name suggests not only Jane Austen's Emma, but Thomas Hardy's first wife, Emma Lavinia Gifford. Emma had turned to the writing of historical novels because it was a way of getting published. She had made the novels more 'romantic' than her natural inclination.

Note that Barbara made her heroine do what she herself could not do – change her style to please the public. Later Barbara thought 'Emma had better be an anthropologist living in the village.' She probably felt on safer ground with an anthropologist.

> She used to live with a man in London? What was the man? Somebody who has been in Africa perhaps, now settled in a provincial university? Occasional appearance on TV as African 'expert.' Perhaps the mother had this cottage.

Now the notes begin to sound like the outline of *A Few Green Leaves*. As Barbara said, 'A microcosm of a village with very little plot,' and she continued to make notes on characters and situations:

> Dr William Gellibrand (Brother of Father G). [Originally Fr Gellibrand was to be an important character, but he simply got a mention in the novel as Harry Gellibrand, the doctor's younger brother.]
>
> Dr Martin Shrubsole and wife Gillian or Gabrielle, who have come from Islington. [She became Avice, of course, a name never before suggested.]
>
> Clergyman Rev. Tim or Ben Dagnell or Doggett, a widower with remote children [he became Tom Dagnell, a childless widower]
>
> His sister Chloe/Kate [renamed Daphne]
>
> Emma Howick or Howard

Her mother Mrs Beatrix (not Trixy) Howick

...the doctor's surgery is crowded but the vicar's study is empty. And there could be a sort of rivalry between them when it comes to dealing with life's difficulties – the vicar cannot write a prescription. In the village there is an elderly woman, weather-beaten by the suns of many years, whose thoughts are always on past Greek holidays – and now perhaps pre-occupied only with hedgehogs.

She [i.e. Emma, the heroine] comes to the village and this former lover appears and is rather troublesome. The Vicar's sister leaves him, so perhaps they could get together? He had better be quite attractive then?

They find an elderly woman wandering in the woods and here the rivalry between vicar and doctor comes out

Further jottings:

The Good Food Guide man; Daphne Dagnall leaving the Rectory; Emma's debacle with the old lover; Tom discovers Emma in the church getting material for her novel - their first real encounter. Miss Lickerish can die. Mrs Dyer's son, 'antique dealer', clearing houses for 'deceased's effects', leaving his card at the door.

'I must have an organist in my next, being paid in bottles of sherry left at his door', wrote Barbara. And later,

Paul Binding and a friend came to dinner, and they drank some of the apricot brandy left over from two years ago. Which leaves me to think that the organist in my new novel might be presented with a bottle of apricot brandy.

The book was finally assembled early in 1979. Between these notes and the final draft, I only found one partial draft of *A Few Green Leaves*, typed on the back of old International African Institute carbon copies, much of it rather faint, which only goes up to the finding of Miss Scudamore (Miss Vereker) in the woods. Presumably other intermediate drafts were destroyed. By this time Barbara was very ill, and progress with the retyping took a long time. On 1 May 1979 she wrote: 'Typing the new novel slowly – have only done 63 pages.'

Hazel Holt wrote in *A Lot To Ask*: 'Barbara sent the manuscript of *A Few Green Leaves* to Macmillan, not really satisfied with it, but knowing that she could now do no more. When I saw her just before Christmas she asked, in her usual practical way, if I would see it through the press for her.'

After the success of *Quartet in Autumn* and *The Sweet Dove Died*, Macmillan were eager to publish this new novel, and on 16 July 1981 James Wright sent a telegram to Hilary: 'The tree is in full leaf.'

If, as is likely, *The Times* was the first newspaper Hilary read on the day after *A Few Green Leaves* was published, she would have been rather disappointed, on Barbara's behalf, with Elaine Feinstein's review.

> 'Sexual intercourse began in 1963
> (which was rather late for me) –
> Between the end of the *Chatterley* ban
> And the Beatles' first LP.'

Alas that the *Annus Mirabilis* Larkin records so ruefully must also have been responsible, at least in part, for the wilderness to which Barbara Pym was relegated for 16 years, and from which, indeed, she only emerged for a brief span of recognition before her death this year. For the passions that spin her plots are smaller, meaner, and in many ways *nastier*, than the jaunty sexuality of that now almost forgotten decade…I confess to coming to Miss Pym's novels late; and my favourite among them is *The Sweet Dove Died*, where the chaste intimacy between a middle-aged woman and a much younger man is analysed with a subtle awareness of all the jealous possessiveness that can lie even in friendships with no apparent sexual base. *A Few Green Leaves* charts altogether more familiar territory, and is unquestionably damaged by doing so; the English Village over which Barbara Pym directs her snide and beady gaze, has been populated by flower-arranging fanatics, cardiganed ladies dreaming of Greece, and hearty GPs as far back as Agatha Christie; and Barbara Pym's peculiarly saddened vision of humanity is overlaid by a lavender-polished patina we never break through for long…

Miss Feinstein admits that there are marvellous moments of comedy, such as 'Daphne's eager announcement "Did you know that a fox's dung is grey and pointed at both ends?" Of which Miss Pym remarks "Nobody did know, and it seemed difficult to follow such a stunning piece of information."'

But this is not sufficient for her to avoid the conclusion that, 'For the sake of Miss Pym's posthumous reputation new readers should decidedly start with the early novels.'

As is the case with most books, the reviews of *A Few Green Leaves* were mixed, the reviewers taking contradictory stances; many of them were not at all complimentary, and some were disappointed that the book did not come up to the standard of earlier works.

On 31 July Alan Kersey of *The Cambridge Evening News* said:

> Sadly the late Barbara Pym did not do anything for her reputation with *A Few Green Leaves* – a big let-down after the practically faultless *The Sweet Dove Died*.

And on 2 August Allan Massie of *The Scotsman* wrote almost the same thing:

> It should be said at once that *A Few Green Leaves* does nothing to support [her] reputation. It is slow and slight, certainly inferior to *The Sweet Dove Died*, its immediate predecessor.

However, a reviewer in a New Zealand publication took the opposite view: 'Her last book further enhances her reputation – devotees of Barbara Pym will not be disappointed in her last novel.'

Rachel Billington in *The Financial Times*, on 2 August, thought:

> Perhaps because there is lassitude at the centre, *A Few Green Leaves* is sadly not such a rich book as earlier works. There is a lack of vitality which in the end cannot be compensated for by any amount of careful analysis.

And Nicholas Shrimpton, in *The New Statesman* on 15 August: 'Slight-ness is all, at least for the Barbara Pym enthusiast, and her final novel has it in abundance.'

Of the United States reviewers, Ann Clark heads her piece in the *Los Angeles Times* on 12 October 'Posthumous disappointment from Pym', and ends her review with 'Sadly this book is unlikely to enhance the reputation of Barbara Pym.'

And Deborah Ovedoff in *The Bulletin* on 16 November thought that 'Despite the author's affection for her people, they emerge as plastic, flat cut-outs, difficult to believe in and really rather dull…'

Michele Slung, in *The Washington Post*, 12 October, sighed, 'One could wish that the last Pym had more of the sparkle of the first books.'

And from *Kirkus Reviews* on 15 July:

> With neither the smiling, sharp edges of the early work nor the perfectly controlled pathos of *Quartet in Autumn*, this is minor Pym – really just a neutral-toned catchall of her acute angles on loneliness and the ravages of time-marching-on…

I should perhaps mention here that *A Few Green Leaves* was only the fifth novel to be published in the US at that time.

Now that Barbara had passed away, one of her reviewers was more open in his criticism of her work than he had previously been. Francis King wrote a review headed 'Fairly Excellent Women' in *The Spectator* on 19 July which started by saying that while he has always admired Barbara Pym, he disputes some comments that have been made about her.

> One reads that she was 'an important novelist', that *A Glass of Blessings* and *Excellent Women* were 'the finest examples of high comedy to have appeared in England during the past 75 years' and that she had 'the wit and style of a 20th century Jane Austen'. In fact, none of these claims can really be substantiated. As a novelist Barbara Pym has about the same importance as E.H. Young, Elizabeth Taylor or Angela Thirkell – to all of whom she bears resemblances; from Saki or Noel Coward there have been many finer examples of high comedy than hers in the last 75 years; and to say that she had the style and wit of a 20th

century Jane Austen is about as accurate as to say that Dodie Smith had the wit and style of a 20th century Congreve. Barbara Pym was a good novelist – which, God knows, is rare -- but she was not an outstanding one. The book is beautifully shaped; every character is distinct; and there is not a page that is not irradiated with wit and fun. Here, for some of our more self-important novelists, is an object-lesson in the advantage of knowing one's limitations and never for a moment attempting to exceed them.

The comparison with Jane Austen was also refuted by Nina Bawden in the *Daily Telegraph* on 17 July: 'I would have admired *A Few Green Leaves* more if Miss Pym's admirers had not likened her to Jane Austen, a comparison that seemed to me a case of overkill.'

And by Allan Massie in *The Scotsman* on 2 August:

[The prose] is disastrous: self-conscious, whimsical, coy; anything further removed from the defining precision of Jane Austen it would be hard to imagine.

Nicholas Shrimpton agreed: '[her] strict social and geographical limitation has at times prompted comparisons with Jane Austen...[but] where Austen was a Romantic miniaturist, Pym is a 20th century minimalist.'

Eve Auchinloss, in the *New York Times Book Review* on 1 January 1981, wrote,

Hearing one more English woman novelist compared to Jane Austen, the reader may feel like reaching for his gun. Barbara Pym often suffered from this light-minded comparison...

But Nina King, reviewing together *A Few Green Leaves* and *Less Than Angels* in *Newsday* on 8 February 1981, said

An English writer of middle class social comedies who names one character after Emma Woodhouse and likens another to the heroine of *Persuasion* invites comparison with Jane Austen. In the case of Barbara Pym, the invitation may be accepted with pleasure. Like Austen, Pym is a meticulous worker in miniature, depicting the everyday concerns of a small group of people...the two writers share, as well, an implicit sense of limitations, an awareness that most people rarely approach either the transcendental heights or the existential abyss.

The comparison with Agatha Christie was noted also by Nina Bawden:

> Although *A Few Green Leaves* is funny, the humour is too often arch or coy instead of deadly, and the way the characters are sketched as types and not developed reminded me more of Agatha Christie. Indeed, as my attention wandered sometimes, it occurred to me that this pleasant rambling tale could have done with a Miss Marple. Murder would have given a sharper focus than lazy Emma's sociological study.

The comparison with Angela Thirkell made by Francis King was echoed by Allan Massie:

> This book suggests where Miss Pym really belonged: with novelists like Angela Thirkell, someone to read while you are eating muffins. Of course, that may be how Mr Larkin and Lord David liked to read novels.

Several reviewers commented on the lack of action in the novel. Allan Massie again: 'The action is minimal...but that could be all right. Incident itself is not necessarily important in a novel. What is important is the quality of the prose, and here it is disastrous...'

Auberon Waugh, a novelist in his own right, and a bit of a show-off – James Wright thought him 'a very silly man' – wrote in the *Evening Standard*:

> Very little happens in Miss Pym's village, and those who are not already captivated by her pointless dialogue and aimless plot construction may find this last novel rather heavy going.

Ann Clark wrote:

> There is no reason at all why a novel with so slight a story line should not succeed, and indeed many purists would consider this absence of adventure a positive merit. But such a novel has to depend particularly heavily on characterisation. Here, unfortunately, Pym fails...

And Nicholas Shrimpton again: 'Plot itself is pared to the bone. What happens in *A Few Green Leaves*? Well, almost nothing...'

Bernard Levin in the *Sunday Times* on 17 July – to whom I shall be returning later – was of a similar opinion:

> ...it is not a lack of interesting events that I am complaining about, for another book I reviewed recently suffered from a similar shortage of drama, yet retained its interest throughout. The additional and dismaying shortage in this book is of any interest in the feelings, attitudes and personalities of the characters and the relationships between them.

The portrayal of Emma also received some criticism. Ann Clark thought she was unconvincing, the Kirkus reviewer called her 'a half-sketched heroine', and Michael Lodico, writing in the Greensboro North Carolina *Daily Record* on 17 May 1981, thought

> Emma herself is the weakest thing in the novel. The most liberated of Pym's women, she is also her dullest...she never really seems to come alive, but remains in the background of the book, rather drab and dim.

Perhaps the most controversial of the reviews was that by Bernard Levin in the *Sunday Times*. Levin was a suave, sophisticated, urban type, and one wonders why he chose, or was chosen, to review a book so far out of his usual orbit; maybe he just wanted to go on one of the ego trips for which he was famed:

> The Barbara Pym story is a strange one. Having written in the 1960s half a dozen novels that appear to have caused no stir, she then disappeared from literary view until the late '70s, when she published two more, and almost overnight became a kind of cult object, compared to Jane Austen. This book is now posthumously published. It is the first of her novels I have read, and unless it is very untypical of her work, I cannot for the life of me understand what all the fuss was about. *A Few Green Leaves* seems to me thin, dull and very nearly pointless.

He goes on to admit a few good points about the book – freedom from clichés, gentle irony, dry wit – but with this faint praise he seems only to damn the book more. Next he describes the characters, asserting that

The real trouble is that these characters cannot think of anything to do. It is not just a question of plot, though as a matter of fact Miss Pym cannot think of anything for them to do either…Moreover there is a kind of nervous underlining in Miss Pym's style that has a rapidly anaesthetic effect; she is rarely content to let the dog see the rabbit, but is constantly clutching the beast by the collar and drawing its attention to the prey…

A Few Green Leaves is nowhere actively bad, boring or offensive. Nor, however, is it anywhere near strong enough, vivid enough or demanding enough to make any difference to anybody. For some it may well succeed in portraying the Heart of England; for me, I fear, it did little but reinforce my long-held belief that the best thing we could do with the countryside is to cover it with an even layer of asphalt.

Preposterous man! Betty Harvey, Henry's sister, was furious when she wrote to Hilary a few days after the review: 'What a brute Bernard Levin is! I was shocked to read his stupid review in *The Sunday Times*. Why should he choose to review it at length when he has read none of her other books. I suppose he just wanted to show off.' We have to agree there.

But not all the reviews were so negative. Even most of the critics I have already mentioned had nice things to say too. Nina Bawden, although objecting to the comparison with Jane Austen, was of the opinion that

A posthumous novel by Barbara Pym is obviously to be welcomed. She writes agreeably, in nice clear prose, and even if the people she writes about are fictionally conventional, she observes them with a careful, mannered irony…An easy read and I enjoyed it.

And, despite her reservations, Rachel Billington in *The Financial Times* on 2 August thought that 'her sense of humour is as strong as ever and this goes a long way to diverting attention from any inadequacies.'

The Kirkus reviewer admitted that 'Readers with the appropriate expectations will find it quietly exact, gently amusing, and (except for that dubious happy ending) genteelly heartbreaking.'

Michele Slung, who thought the book lacked sparkle, makes the interesting point that

> Emma Howick is the first of the major Pym female characters
> to be an intellectual, though some of the secondary ones – notably Helena Napier and Sybil Forsyth – in previous books had
> careers in anthropology and archaeology. Up to Emma, Pym's
> central women have each emphasized their own lack of seriousness...Somehow Emma is an amalgam of all Pym's heroines,
> the place at which they all meet. Not as sleek as Wilmet, she is
> not as depressing as *Quartet's* Marcia either. Self-absorbed, but
> without Leonora's solipsism...One of Pym's talents, it seems, is
> for revealing her characters on two levels – how they see themselves and how they are seen by others.

Eve Auchinloss: 'she surprises comedy and sadness from the most banal
and cosy moments without ever managing to be dull.'

A small handful of reviewers had nothing but praise for *A Few Green
Leaves*. Geoffrey Trease, in the December issue of *British Book News*,
thought that 'Though this posthumous book is most regrettably her
last, its quality can be rated emphatically Pym's No. 1.'

And the Otago *Daily Times* (Dunedin, NZ) reviewer on 22 April 1981
proudly asserted

> It may here be remarked that long before Philip Larkin and
> Lord David Cecil told the British reading public that Barbara
> Pym's was an undeservedly neglected talent, the staff of the
> Dunedin Public Library in the late 50s and early 60s recognised and relished each new Pym as it appeared.

Maureen T. Reddy in the *Minnesota Daily* on 21 October was enthusiastic:

> She excels at uncovering many levels of unexpected meaning in
> the quiet lives she writes about and clearly takes great pleasure
> in what she finds. *A Few Green Leaves* may well be Pym's finest
> work...

Gloria Whelan for the Detroit Free Press wrote on 16 November 1980:

Ever since Cranford there has been a fascination for novels about the goings-on in small English villages...but none approaches Pym's observations of man's funny and pathetically brave efforts to live up to the ill-founded rumour that he is a social animal.

Barbara's long time admirer, A. N. Wilson, writing in *The Times Literary Supplement* on 18 July, said

In tone and setting, *A Few Green Leaves* goes back to the comic atmosphere of *Some Tame Gazelle*, but the realism is sharper, the underlying poignancy more carefully implied. Reading it, one gets the best of both the early and the late Pym manner; a full and distinctive taste of what her novels are like.

And Paul Bailey, in *The Observer*, 27 July.

Although Barbara Pym completed *A Few Green Leaves* some months before her death earlier this year, the novel shows no signs of having been written against the clock. It is notable, rather, for the quiet confidence of its unhurried narrative, which accommodated a dozen or so sharply differentiated characters in a beguiling manner...Emma, like her creator, is a meticulous chronicler of bring-and-buy sales, church fetes, parish council meetings. For Barbara Pym's art thrives on just such non epoch-making events.

A very perceptive review by Peter Kemp in *The Listener* on 17 July emphasises Pym's near obsession with death and its trappings.

The book is packed with calmly contemplated intimations of mortality. A village graveyard and a family mausoleum figure prominently in the narrative. A widowed vicar, interested in local history, keenly rummages through 17th century edicts about 'burying in woollen', elderly female parishioners cheerily frequent the churchyard, studying gravestones and deciphering epitaphs. There is casual joking about an old-age pensioner who dies during a charabanc sing-song. One of the novel's older ladies is teasingly brought to the point of what seems to be her death, and then reprieved; while the death of another is sprung upon the reader with sudden cold effectiveness: 'the cat left her and sought the warmth of his basket, Miss Lickerish's lap having become strangely chilled'....The book's attitude to death is cheerfully down-to-earth. It's response to life is one of slightly melancholy irony. Keeping going on substitutes and second-bests, the majority of its characters have been disappointed but are not dispirited. The ability to find consolations for emotional lack always fascinates Miss Pym...This is the third excellent novel to appear since Barbara Pym's Indian summer as a novelist began in 1977. Filled with symptoms of change and decay, it also includes heartening instances of end-of-season blooming...Emma finally turns out to be one of Barbara Pym's late-flowering spinsters: after an old relationship has shown itself incapable of sprouting into much, a new one buds promisingly - as this novel stocked with seasonal imagery ends.

The other category of critical material on which I have drawn in previous papers like this, are congratulatory letters from friends and fans, but of course, since Barbara had died before publication, there are very few of these; I found just three letters from 'fans' who were not aware that Barbara had died, and none referred to the book in question.

If the selection I have made from the many reviews Barbara received for this book from distinguished writers in national newspapers, and lesser luminaries on local papers, are representative of the general opinion, I have to conclude reluctantly that Barbara's literary life ended with a whimper, rather than a bang. But as Barbara herself admitted, when she was laboriously retyping her novel in 1979, 'Some people may be disappointed in this – others will like it.'

An earler version of this paper was presented at the 2009 North American Conference in Cambridge, Massachusetts.

14

Epilogue

After having published seven novels and written
a great many more, I suppose I can be said to have found
a voice of sorts. I hope so, anyway... I think that's
the kind of immortality most authors would want –
to feel that their work would be immediately recognisable
as having been written by them and by nobody else.

14

Epilogue

In spite of the lukewarm reception I have suggested for Barbara's last novel, *A Few Green Leaves*, the interest shown by Pym readers had not in the least abated. Macmillan seemed prepared to publish the remaining several novels and many short stories, and to this end Barbara's literary executor, Hazel Holt, set about editing and completing a number of these.

An Unsuitable Attachment, written after *No Fond Return of Love*, was abruptly, almost brutally, rejected by Cape in March 1964, and submission to many other publishers (sometimes under the title *Wrapped in Lemon Leaves*) was also unsuccessful. Hazel made a few minor deletions ('though nothing, of course, has been added'[1]) and the novel was published in 1982.

The next posthumous Pym appeared in 1985, the very early (1938-9) *Crampton Hodnet*. At the outbreak of the Second World War Barbara had to put writing aside as she embarked on various wartime activities, culminating in service in the WRNS (Women's Royal Naval Service). Reappraising it after the war, Barbara decided that it was outdated, and never offered it to any publisher, but used some of its characters in subsequent published novels. Hazel says in her prefatory note:

> *Crampton Hodnet* is one of Barbara's earliest completed novels, and in it she was still feeling her way as a writer. Occasional over-writing and over-emphasis led to repetition, which, in preparing the manuscript for press, I have tried to eliminate. I was greatly helped by Barbara's own emendations (made in the 1950s) and by some notes she made about this novel in her pocket diary for 1939...Barbara herself lit upon the exact word to describe this book. It is more purely funny than any of her later novels. So far, everyone who has read the manuscript has laughed out loud – even in the Bodleian Library.[2]

Early in 1970, after *The Sweet Dove Died* had been rejected several times, Barbara made a start on a new novel, apparently inspired by an academic argument in an article in *Africa*, the anthropological journal of which she was Assistant Editor.

In June 1971 she wrote to Philip Larkin:

> Rather to my surprise I find that I have nearly finished the first draft of another novel about a provincial university told by the youngish wife of a lecturer. It was supposed to be a sort of Margaret Drabble effort, but of course it hasn't turned out like that at all.

Writing to Bob Smith a few months later she said 'I have finished the first draft of a novel about a provincial university...two characters in it rather like Richard and his mother, exiles from the Caribbean. Perhaps my immediate circle of friends will like to read it.' But in May the next year she wrote to Philip Larkin: 'I have been too busy or too lazy or too discouraged to go on with my provincial university novel... ' and in October: 'I tinker with my provincial university novel sometimes. Next year, when I'm due to retire I shall have more time.'

Barbara was not really satisfied with this novel, to which she never gave a title, and she never revised it, instead turning her attention to the construction of *Quartet in Autumn*.

Barbara left two drafts of the 'academic novel', one in the first person. Hazel Holt prepared this novel for publication by amalgamating the two drafts, 'also making use of some notes that she made and consulting the original handwritten version, trying to "smooth" them (to use Barbara's word) into a coherent whole. This version does, I hope, restore the Pym voice.'[3] She also added the title *An Academic Question*.

Hazel said that 'when Barbara wrote this book...she had no real expectation of its ever being published'.[3] Thanks to Hazel's assiduous work this novel was eventually published in 1986.

Hazel's last effort to bring to the public all of Barbara's unpublished work that she considered worthy was *Civil to Strangers and Other Writings*. The title story was Barbara's second novel, written in 1936. The 'other writings' mostly date from the late 1930s and early forties, and consist of the short novel *Gervase and Flora,* two wartime novels (one unfinished), four short stories, two of which had already been published elsewhere, and the 1978 radio talk *Finding a Voice.*

After the publication of *Civil to Strangers* in 1987 Hazel felt that she had completed her task. Both she and Hilary Pym Walton were adamant that unfinished, sub-standard, and immature works should not be published merely because of the fame of their author.[4] Since then Hazel has approved the printing of four more short stories in the Barbara Pym Society's newsletter *Green Leaves,* and more unpublished material has been presented as dramatic readings at the Society's Oxford conferences.

By the 1990s many if not all Barbara's novels were out of print, but since 2007 Virago has reprinted nearly all of them in England, each with a foreword by a distinguished author. The novels are also being re-issued in the U.S. in time for the Pym centenary in 2013, and they are also available as e-book digital downloads. The steady demand for her books and the enthusiasm of her devoted readers suggests that Barbara's work will not again be easily forgotten.

Sources and Notes

Primary Sources

University of Oxford, Bodleian Library. Catalogue of the papers of Barbara Mary Crampton Pym (1913-80). Shelfmarks MSS. Pym 1-178.

Holt, Hazel and Pym, Hilary (eds.) *A Very Private Eye: The Diaries, Letters and Notebooks of Barbara Pym*. London: Macmillan, 1984.

Holt, Hazel. *A Lot to Ask: A Life of Barbara Pym*. London: Macmillan, 1990.

Notes

Chapter 1
[1]Lewis, Roy, and Foy, Yvonne. *The British in Africa*. London: Weidenfeld and Nicolson, 1971, p 218.

Chapter 2
[1]Wyatt-Brown, Anne M. *Barbara Pym: A Critical Biography*. Columbia, MO, University of Missouri Press, 1992.

Chapter 3
[1]Conford, Philip. A Forum for Organic Husbandry: The *New English Weekly* and Agricultural Policy, 1939-1949. *The Agricultural History Review* (1998) Vol. 46 No. 2, p 200

Chapter 4
Readers' Digest. *The Fragile Peace 1919-1939: The Years Between the Wars*. London: Readers' Digest, 1998.

Chapter 5
[1]Meek, Charles Kingsley. *A Sudanese kingdom: an ethnographical study of the Jukun-speaking peoples of Nigeria*. With introduction by H. R. Palmer. London: K. Paul, Trench, Trübner & Co., 1931.

Chapter 6
[1]Liddell, Robert. *A Mind at Ease: Barbara Pym and Her Novels.* London: Peter Owen, 1989, p. 38.

[2]Long, Robert Emmet. *Barbara Pym.* New York: Ungar, 1986, p. 59.

Chapter 8
[1]Pym, Barbara. 'Ups and Downs of a Writer's Life.' Typescript of talk to Senior Wives Fellowship, United Reformed Church, Headington, Oxford, with manuscript annotations, 1978. MS. Pym 98:79-83

Chapter 10
[1]Holt, Hazel. *A Lot to Ask.* London: Macmillan, 1990, p. 179

[2]Liddell, Robert, op. cit., p. 88

[3]*Green Leaves*, 4(1) 1998, p. 7

Chapter 12
[1]Holt, Hazel, op. cit., p. 258

[2]Letter to Philip Larkin, 1977, quoted by Hazel Holt, op. cit., p. 261

[3]Snow, Lotus. In Salwak, Dale, ed. *The Life and Work of Barbara Pym.* Iowa City: University of Iowa Press, 1987, pp. 120-121

[4]Ackley, Katherine A. *The Novels of Barbara Pym.* New York: Garland, 1989

[5]Long, Robert Emmet. *Barbara Pym.* New York: Ungar, 1986, p. 188

[6]Liddell, Robert, op. cit., p. 122

Epilogue
[1]Pym, Barbara. *An Unsuitable Attachment.* London: Macmillam, 1982. Literary Executor's note.

[2]Pym, Barbara. *Crampton Hodnet.* London: Macmillam, 1985, p. vi.

[3]Pym, Barbara. *An Academic Question.* London: Macmillan, 1986. Prefatory note by Hazel Holt.

[4]Personal communication.

Books about Barbara Pym

Ackley, Katherine Anne. *The Novels of Barbara Pym.* Garland Publishing, 1989

Allen, Orphia Jane. *Barbara Pym: Writing A Life.* Scarecrow Press, 1994

Bell, Hazel K., ed. *No Soft Incense: Barbara Pym and the Church.* The Barbara Pym Society, 2004

Benet, Diana. *Something to Love: Barbara Pym's Novels.* University of Missouri Press, 1986

Burkhart, Charles. *The Pleasure of Miss Pym.* University of Texas Press, 1987

Cooley, Mason. *The Comic Art of Barbara Pym.* AMS Studies in Modern Literature, AMS Press, 1990

Cotsell, Michael. *Barbara Pym.* Modern Novelists, Palgrave Macmillan, 1989

Donato, Deborah. *Reading Barbara Pym.* Fairleigh Dickinson University Press, 2005

Garner, Lawrence. *Oswestry Girl: Barbara Pym 1913-1980.* Oswestry and District Civic Society, 2005

Holt, Hazel. *A Lot to Ask: A Life of Barbara Pym.* E. P. Dutton, 1990

Hunting, Constance. *One Little Room an Everywhere: The Novels of Barbara Pym.* Puckerbrush Press, 1987

Lenckos, Frauke Elisabeth and Miller, Ellen J., eds. *'All This Reading': The Literary World of Barbara Pym.* Fairleigh Dickinson University Press, 2003

Liddell, Robert. *A Mind at Ease: Barbara Pym and Her Novels.* Peter Owen, 1989

Little, Judy. *The Experimental Self: Dialogic Subjectivity in Woolf, Pym, and Brooke-Rose.* Southern Illinois University Press, 1996

Long, Robert Emmet. *Barbara Pym*. Ungar Publishing, 1986

Nardin, Jane. *Barbara Pym*. Twayne's English Authors Series, Twayne Publishers, 1985

Raz, Orna. *Social Dimensions in the Novels of Barbara Pym, 1949-1963: The Writer as Hidden Observer*. Mellen Press, 2007

Rossen, Janice. *The World of Barbara Pym*. Palgrave Macmillan, 1987

Rossen, Janice, ed. *Independent Women: The Function of Gender in the Novels of Barbara Pym*. St Martin's Press, 1988

Salwak, Dale, ed. *The Life and Work of Barbara Pym*. University of Iowa Press, 1987

Salwak, Dale. *Barbara Pym: A Reference Guide*. Reference Publications in Literature, G. K. Hall, 1991

Solow, Harrison. *Felicity and Barbara Pym*. Cinnamon Press, 2010

Tsagaris, Ellen M. *The Subversion of Romance in the Novels of Barbara Pym*. University of Wisconsin Press, 1998

Weld, Annette. *Barbara Pym and the Novel of Manners*. Palgrave Macmillan, 1992

Wyatt-Brown, Anne M. *Barbara Pym: A Critical Biography*. University of Missouri Press, 1992

Index

Abbreviations used in the index are: BP for Barbara Pym; BPS for the Barbara Pym Society; IAI for the International African Institute; *AQ* for *An Academic Question*; *CH* for *Crampton Hodnet*; *EW* for *Excellent Women*; *GB* for *A Glass of Blessings*; *JP* for *Jane and Prudence*; *LTA* for *Less than Angels*; *NFR* for *No Fond Return of Love*; *QA* for *Quartet in Autumn*; *STG* for *Some Tame Gazelle*; *SDD* for *The Sweet Dove Died*; *UA* for *An Unsuitable Attachment*; *VPE* for *A Very Private Eye*.

Novels by Barbara Pym are entered under their titles; works by other writers are entered under the authors' names. Letters written by Barbara Pym are entered under the names of their recipients.